DIARY OF A
F.A.T.
(FED UP AND TIRED)
GIRL

TANISHA THOMAS

A POST HILL PRESS BOOK
ISBN (hardcover): 978-1-61868-929-0
ISBN (eBook): 978-1-61868-930-6

DIARY OF A F.A.T. (FED UP AND TIRED) GIRL
© 2016 by Tanisha Thomas
All Rights Reserved

Post Hill Press
275 Madison Avenue, 14th Floor
New York, NY 10016
http://posthillpress.com

CONTENTS

Prologue   F.A.T. Doesn't Mean What You Think It Does..................................1

Chapter 1   First Love, Or Sometimes You Need To Slap A Bitch..............................5
Chapter 2   Bad To The Bone...9
Chapter 3   Pulling Punches, Smashing Pots And Pans.................................17
Chapter 4   The Godmother of All Bad Girls...22
Chapter 5   Controlled Chaos: The BGC Reunions.....................................26
Chapter 6   "Larger Than Life" Is A Euphemism......................................33
Chapter 7   The Devil Doesn't Only Wear Prada......................................40
Chapter 8   The Groupie Life...44
Chapter 9   Ménage À Trois..54
Chapter 10   Tanisha Gets Divorced (Well, She Tries To).............................62
Chapter 11   Looking For The One...Or One Who Will Pay For Dinner....................71
Chapter 12   Catfished...79
Chapter 13   Tips From The Dating Trenches...85
Chapter 14   Money And Envy..89
Chapter 15   The Best Show I Ever Hosted, On The Worst Day Of My Life...............97
Chapter 16   BFFs Forever...103
Chapter 17   Thirty Days—and a Lifetime—to a Better Me.............................109
Chapter 18   Rules To Live By...116
Chapter 19   The (Mostly) Happy Ending..118

About the Author...123

PROLOGUE

F.A.T. Doesn't Mean What You Think It Does

Dear Diary,

What the hell did I do to deserve this?
I'm so fuckin' done.
—Tanisha

I was twenty years old when I flew in a plane for the first time. It was the summer of 2005 and I was headed to Los Angeles to film *Bad Girls Club*. I was convinced that I had finally gotten my big break. As I boarded the plane in New York I thought, *I, Tanisha Thomas, am going to Hollywood and I am never coming back...*

I'll be honest, my imagination really ran wild. By the time we touched down at LAX I had envisioned it all: I'd be a Hollywood starlet with the paparazzi always on her heels, a HOT and sizzling "damn he's fine" man by my side, two kids, and a Shih Tzu that I'd carry around in a designer purse. The vision was oh so crystal clear. I'd be filthy rich, successful and, most importantly, I'd be in love.

And for once in my life I'd be in shape, sexy and fit. Did I forget to mention fit?

I was so excited I nearly skipped and twirled off the plane. Are you rolling your eyes yet? Well, bear with me. I can't help it. You see, I'm a Virgo, so my success is written in the stars. I mean, don't hate the girl, honey, hate the horoscope. The Universe wants me to be rich and famous! I'm driven to perfection and fabulousness, and I'm persistent and ambitious. Once I put my mind to something, that is it!

That's it, right? Well, all these years later, let's check in with my progress on the amazing "vision" I once had:

Career: I'm never ever satisfied, and work can never seem to come in steady or fast enough. But, I'll give this one a check.

Weight: Still doubling down on the Spanx, sometimes tripling (depending on what I ate that week) but at least my hair and make up is always laid for the gods!

Fine ass man: Um, does my vibrator count?

Two kids: You know what? I think we can stop now.

I'm convinced that my life is one big Lifetime movie and I have the lead role—even though I never auditioned. I am telling you, you simply can't make none of this shit up! My life is so crazy it makes *Dawson's Creek* look like a children's lullaby.

Here I am, nearing thirty, still at home, my husband ducking and dodging the divorce papers like they're the plague. I'm barely eating but the scale refuses to move, and I'm running into my neighbors—some of who are married by the way—and all my exes on the dating sites! Oh, and I still don't have any kids (smh). Did I forget to mention that part?

For someone that always seems to have the master plan, my life never goes as expected. Mind you, it's not just about me not having kids. It's about that twenty-year-old girl in a plane for the first time, riding high off the feeling that her first big break would mean a lifetime of love, happiness, and success. And now, years later, nothing in my life is happening quite the way I thought it would. From my family driving me insane to picking up the damn check almost every time I go on a date, from facing the dreaded scale day after day, and seeking acceptance in the public eye, I'm fed up and tired. F.A.T.

I'm tired of complaining, though, and I'm sure you're already tired of hearing it. Which is why it's a good thing for both of us that every obstacle I've encountered has made me a better person—and I'm thankful for that. I may not have reached the milestones with my career and family that I thought I would at this age, but mentally and emotionally, I'm light years ahead.

I'm here to tell you that there's no handbook for this thing called life. Screw what it's supposed to be like and learn to roll with the punches. What screws us up is not what happens to us—it's that picture we keep in our minds of what it all should look like.

When life throws you lemons…throw that crap back and demand chocolate, dammit! Nothing is going to go as planned. All you can hope is to still have your hairline and be "better" not "bitter."

I'm so different from the woman I was last year, and the year before that. Five years ago I would have probably punched you in the mouth if you offended me, now you'd be lucky if I responded. It took a lot of work to get here. A lot of work, and a whole lot of drama.

So buckle your seatbelts, and get ready to learn from all of my mishaps and mistakes! If I could save at least one of you the trouble then maybe just maybe it was all worth it.

CHAPTER 1

First Love, Or Sometimes You Need To Slap A Bitch

This may come as a shock to you, but I've never been one to hold my tongue.

My dad, on the other hand, rarely showed raw emotion, so when I was in the third grade I was surprised to come home one day and find him heartbroken over my broken piggy bank.

It was Valentine's Day and I'd decided to go all out on the love of my eight year-old life: Raymond Taylor. Raymond was fine! He was an athlete, and he had nice, caramel skin, big brown eyes, and full, perfect lips. All the girls liked him, and I knew I needed to go all out to prove that I was destined to be Mrs. Raymond Taylor.

You're probably thinking that I wrote Raymond a nice little Valentine card, or slipped him one of those notes asking, "Do you like me? Check 'yes' or 'no.'"

Well you're wrong. I cashed in my life savings.

Were you paying attention during the prologue? I wasn't kidding when I told you I was determined.

I'd kept a ceramic piggy bank on my dresser, a pink pig with a ballerina skirt and a crown that contained all the allowance and birthday money I'd ever earned or received over the years. I tried to shake the money out of it but when that didn't work, I smashed the damn thing! Then I waltzed my little butt down to the drug store (while my school driver waited for me outside) and bought a giant box of chocolates and the biggest teddy bear I could find!

When I returned home, arms full of Valentine's Day bounty, I found my dad sweeping up the remnants of my piggy bank. He eyed me up and down, looking distraught.

"Daddy, what's wrong?" I asked, totally clueless.

"Baby," he said, voice quivering. "Did you spend all your money on those presents? Who are they for?"

"Raymond Taylor," I said, smiling from ear to ear.

He lost it. My reserved, soft-spoken dad was crushed.

"Daddy," I pressed him. "What's wrong?"

Then he spoke the words that would haunt me until this very day. The prophecy, the curse, whatever you want to call it.

"Men are going to be the death of my little girl. I just know it." I was eight years old going on nine and I had no idea what he meant back then, but boy was I about to find out!

Daddy was right. Don't believe me? Let's skip ahead to the fifth grade and Christopher Johnson. Did I say Raymond Taylor was fine? Well Christopher was super-fine. (And Raymond shared my chocolates with the rest of our fourth grade class, so fuck him). Christopher and I were in a school play together and one day during rehearsals he grabbed my hand and pulled me toward him.

"Hey Tanisha," he whispered. "Do you want to go together?"

"Um, yes!" I replied, bursting with excitement.

So we started going out—whatever that means in fifth grade. God knows, if my mother had found out, she would have beaten the life out of me. But I was happy! I felt like a star. Here was the boy that everyone else wanted, and he wanted me. Plus, I didn't have to spend all my money to get him to be my boyfriend.

But about a week later, I noticed a lot of not-so-discrete whispering and giggling behind my back. Never a good sign.

"Girl, what's going on?" I asked my friend, Felicia.

"I don't know if you know," she said, "But Lucette says she's going out with Christopher."

"No girl," I insisted. "Christopher is MY boyfriend... That would never happen!" Felicia told me not to worry, and that it was probably just a rumor.

But I just had to find out for myself. So that day at lunch, I walked up to Lucette and straight-up asked her. "Lucette, are you going out with Chris?"

She smiled looked up into the ceiling then back at me and shook her head yes. Bitch had some damn nerve stealing my man! I mean we were classmates, wtf?

I started to walk away, but then this rage came over me. I was trembling, I was so angry. So I turned around and smacked her. I mean it wasn't an ordinary slap either, lol. I pretty much back-handed her. Could you believe I was fighting since the fifth grade?

She burst into tears and fled the classroom. While I stood there feeling like Denzel Washington in *Training Day*.

I'd already thought that people were talking shit about me and that cheating son of a bitch Christopher. But after I slapped Lucette, the gossip went to a whole new level! Everyone was talking!

"That's why you can't keep a boyfriend," my classmates told me. "It's because you're crazy."

How is this my fault when he cheated on me? I wondered. *Am I crazy? What's wrong with me?*

I ended up going out with Christopher's best friend a week later. He was cuter anyway.

Here's what I learned. You might be cursed when it comes to love, but you're not helpless. So:

1) Always stand up for yourself. And be prepared to smack a bitch or two.

2) When it doesn't work out, try dating his friend. Or his cousin. At the very least, it'll piss him off beyond belief.

CHAPTER 2

Bad To The Bone

"Save this—one day I'll be famous."

This is how I signed off on every piece of correspondence—every letter, birthday card, maybe even a receipt or two—from the moment I learned to write legibly until the day I taped my first TV show.

Call me cocky, call me an attention whore, but I always knew I had an "it" factor. When I was growing up in Brooklyn, my parents couldn't turn on *Star Search* without having to watch the Tanisha Thomas sideshow. I'd sing, dance, and do cartwheels in the living room. I outshone every motherfucker who competed on that show.

I've always been a creative person. I started writing poetry when I was in third grade, and I was actually really good at it, if I do say so myself. I went through an intense phase of wanting to be a journalist, and I would set up a newsroom in our kitchen, reporting on current events from elementary school.

Breaking news, we ran out of chocolate milk today.

My parents would play along, listening intently and laughing when I cracked jokes. I enjoyed the attention, of course, but I also got a particular thrill out of having an audience and controlling the room. It was all eyes on me—and I wanted to keep it that way.

When I turned twelve, my mom and dad enrolled me in dance and theater classes. It's possible that they just got tired of watching me stage performances all over the house, but whatever their motivation was, I was thrilled. I loved improv—the energy, the spontaneity, having to be witty and think on my feet.

Wit. Hmm…something that would most definitely come in handy later on.

I was so fortunate to have parents that encouraged me at a young age. Well, for the most part anyway. As I got older, though, my relationship with them started to fray—particularly with my mom. Sure, I wasn't an easy teenager. I was determined to do things my own way, and I was stubborn as hell. But my mom was very critical of my appearance and of my willingness to speak my mind. She had a difficult time expressing her feelings and showing emotional support, and while she was willing to pay for acting lessons for a couple of years, she didn't believe that I could really make a career out of it.

When I was in high school, I had the lead role in my very first play, *The Insanity of Mary Girard*. Being on stage for our opening night was such an incredible feeling—I'll never forget it. I had never done anything so energizing and exciting. I had a fire inside me that night, and it showed. I killed it.

I had begged my mom to come to our opening night, but she couldn't get off work. She didn't understand how much the play meant to me—she hadn't been very supportive about it in the weeks leading up to our performance—and it really hurt me that she hadn't tried harder to make it to the show. But as forthcoming as I've always been in all aspects of my life, I couldn't bring myself talk to my mom about it. I tried to play it off like it didn't matter, but my drama teacher and mentor, who directed our play, encouraged me to speak up.

"It's not okay," he said after the play was over. "This is a big deal for you. You need to have a conversation with your family about supporting you."

I considered his advice for a while and decided he was right. When I got home that night, I confronted my mom. Our conversation went nowhere; we ended up getting in a heated argument, and that was that.

The tension between my mom and me got worse over the next year or so. I started acting out. I got a reputation for mouthing off in school, and I became ridiculously boy crazy. It didn't help that I was beautiful, either. Honey, it was a gift and a curse. Perky boobs, nice booty, tiny waist—you couldn't deny it. I even had a teachers flirting with me, at age thirteen! All the boys were looking, especially the bad boys. They liked me best.

That was a fun time.

Then my parents got divorced, and my mom got an awful new boyfriend. I was unhappy and angry at home, and it showed at school. I was unhappy and angry at home, and it showed at school. I started mouthing off, getting in fights, and hanging with the wrong crowd. My mom and I were at each other's throats. Do you think *I'm* strong and opinionated? Well, you should meet my mom. She's very intimidating and aggressive, and she called the shots in our household. She was also a cop, and I learned early on that with a name like Tanisha and a mom who is NYPD, people don't mess with you.

Let's just say I take after her.

But when I was growing up, we didn't see eye to eye. My mom's from Grenada, and coming from a West Indian background, her focus was always family and school first every. Friends weren't even on the list. She didn't understand why I wanted to have a social life. She was always trying to keep me at home, and it made me want to do the opposite.

Despite our very tumultuous relationship, the older I get, the more I realize that I have a lot of my mom's traits. Yeah, we're both strong, outspoken women, but it's more than that. Our attention to detail is insane. We're both the biggest germaphobes you'll ever meet. I hate Band-Aids. If the chair or a couch has a rip in it, I won't even sit on it. I smell like rubbing alcohol because I'm always rubbing my hands with alcohol. My mom is the same way.

If only I was like that with guys and snacks! I would be skinny and I wouldn't have so much drama!

Anyway, by age fourteen I had had it, so I up and moved out. I was convinced I'd never come back. (Story of my life.)

I was on my own for a long time. I lived in the basement of an apartment building with some friends. All I wanted was to find a sugar daddy to take care of me. And it wasn't long before I did. I fell in love, and I thought that I would be set for life. But things didn't work out, unfortunately. I couldn't make ends meet, so at nineteen I had no choice but to move back home. I felt like a failure. When I was still in school, I had teachers telling me that I wouldn't ever make anything of myself. They said I had a bad attitude, and made bad decisions, and that I'd end up on welfare with three kids by the time I was twenty-five. At the time I thought, "You can go fuck yourself." But there I was just a few years later, living in my mom's basement as an adult, after five years of living independently. I ended up with a job as a waitress at Applebee's but they demoted me to takeout server because I was too rude to actually interact with people. I had a boyfriend, Clive (you'll hear more about him later), but not much else going on.

I was depressed.

Then one day, everything changed. I was watching TV on the couch, flipping through the channels, when I saw a casting call for a reality show.

Are you a bad girl?

"Yeah!" I said out loud, chuckling to myself.

Do you do whatever you want?

"Hell yes!" I practically shouted.

Then send us your application for Oxygen's Bad Girls Club...

I had never seen the show and but I thought, "Why the hell not?" and filled out an online questionnaire.

Apparently I wasn't the only one who thought I'd be a good fit. The next day, I was hanging out with two of my friends, and one of them mentioned that he'd submitted an application for a reality show on my behalf.

"What? Which show?" I asked.

"*Bad Girls Club*," he replied.

I couldn't believe it. "Why?"

He laughed. "Tanisha, because you're the definition of a bad girl."

It had been years since my performance in *The Insanity of Mary Girard,* years since I'd thought about being on stage and dreamed of becoming rich and famous. Sitting in my mom's basement, with no clue what I was going to do with my life, I tried not to get my hopes up.

But I'll be honest: I did get my hopes up.

I didn't hear anything from the network for a while, though. I figured it just wasn't meant to be, so I went about my business. Then, after what felt like years, but was probably weeks, I got an email. I was invited to an in-person audition at Chelsea Market in Manhattan! I couldn't believe my luck.

The luck turned out to be temporary. Of course, it was raining cats and dogs the day of my audition and, of course, I got stuck at work and was running late. I sprinted to the subway in the pouring rain, desperately trying to keep my clothes and hair dry. And of course, the train was delayed. When it finally arrived it was so packed full of wet, pissed-off commuters that I had to shove my way into the car.

This is my one chance! Let me on the fucking train! I wanted to scream at everyone.

Fuck it, I might as well be honest. I did scream at everyone.

By the time I got to the studio—soaking wet, my hair and makeup a hot mess, and pissed to high hell about my disastrous train ride—all of the auditions were over. The security guard was about to lock the door.

"DO NOT LOCK THAT DOOR!" I hollered.

He backed up a step, looking terrified, and decided not to argue.

Smart man.

I quickly checked in and burst into the studio. The casting directors were still there, but they were packing up. They looked half-asleep, as if they'd just sat through a long, hard day of hearing crazy bitches mouthing off. Despite my late arrival they agreed to meet with me.

"Tell us about yourself," one of the casting directors said. He couldn't have seemed less interested.

"Okayyyy, but first let me tell you about this damn train ride over here!" I yelled, still struggling to catch my breath. "This bitch had the nerve to take up two seats. Can you believe it?"

They all perked up in their seats, their eyes suddenly bright. It was clear: I had their undivided attention.

After some weeks my first time on a plane when I made it to finals, I got a phone call from the head casting director.

"Hey Tanisha," he said. "I wanted to call to thank you for auditioning. We're very sorry to tell you—"

My heart was in my throat.

"That you won't be spending the summer in New York."

What the fuck?

"You'll be in Los Angeles—"

I leapt up from the couch.

"Taping the *Bad Girls Club*."

Everything was sort of a blur. I was ready and so focused. It was most definitely my time.

CHAPTER 3

Pulling Punches, Smashing Pots And Pans

For the most part, I'm a very private and laid back person. Eighty percent of the time I like to be at home, with my family, kicking back, being quiet and unseen. I don't always need to be the center of attention. At work its a different story... something happens to me when those cameras come on. I instantly come alive!

Now, it's hard to explain what being on a reality show is like, but suffice it to say that on *Bad Girls Club* we had a house full of women who all experienced a similar transformation on camera, for better or for worse. More often than not, for worse.

And the cameras were always on. At least it seemed that way!

When I first met all my roommates in Los Angeles, I kept thinking to myself, *this shit is crazy*. There were seven of us living together in this beautiful house, all very different women from different walks of life—and all kind of nuts, in our own special way. I should point out that the casting for the first few seasons of BGC was a little...flexible. These days they do extensive background checks, but when I was on the show, it was kind of a free for all. These girls weren't aspiring actresses putting on a show, they were just straight up bad. There were no fake storylines and no manufactured drama.

This shit was not watered down.

So there I was in a house with six other Bad Girls. No television, no phones, no radio, no men. Just a lot of anger management issues and a ton of liquor. It was intense. As you probably know by now, I'm not one to start drama, but I'm not afraid to stand up for myself. I wasn't planning on getting to the BCG house and ruffling everyone's feathers just for fun. I was there to enjoy the experience...but at the same time I'm not someone to fuck with. I mean, honey, I'm from Brooklyn. I was raised to keep it real and raw. It's definitely a New York thing!

"Let me tell y'all something," I said in one of my first interviews. "A true bad girl, she doesn't start nothing. She waits till you start. And then, she pops off."

Luckily for our ratings, I didn't have to wait long to pop off.

The very first night in the house, a few of the girls went out drinking and two of them, Cordelia and Darlen, got in a fight. I didn't even go out with them, but when they got home, I heard that they had been throwing around my name. Darlen called me a fat bitch! I couldn't believe it. I had known these girls for eight hours and they were already talking shit about me?

I completely lost my temper.

Ding Ding Ding! Episode One: Tanisha loses her goddamn mind.

After that first night, it really kicked in. This is the Bad Girls Club, I thought. These girls are bad. And I'm even badder.

We shot for two and a half months, which is a really long time for a reality show these days. Most series only film a few weeks for each season. We had a lot of drama, and there were times that I thought, Now this feels like a damn battlefield! THIS house is divided. But in the end, we kind of came together.

Oxygen reported record numbers for Season Two. We were the first show on the network ever to break the one million-viewer mark.

Why? Because it was real. It was as real as real can get, and none of it was manufactured. So many people have told me that they hated reality TV until they watched that season of BGC. The way we acted, the way we dealt with each other, that was all unscripted, edgy and raw. That's why it was such a standout season.

And while there was plenty of yelling and screaming, we weren't allowed to get in physical fights. Our executive producer, Laura, happened to be a psychologist and was a lifesaver for us—and for the network, I'm sure. Every single day when taping ended, she would come off camera and work with us, talk to us.

"You have to find a way to communicate without getting physical," she told us over and over again. "You have to find other ways of dealing with people."

"What?" I blurted out the first time she gave me this advice. "Communicate without being physical? I'm from Brooklyn. What are you talking about?"

Laura insisted that I was smart enough to find a way to express my feelings. While I was clearly skeptical—verbal communication had gotten me nowhere with my mom when I was growing up, and on the streets of Brooklyn it was unheard of—I took her advice to heart.

Well, sort of. You see, I added my own Tanisha twist to her line of thinking. At the very least, I realized, I could find a more creative way to get on the nerves of these bitches and provoke them to hit me first. Then, I'd have an excuse to fight.

Laura, honey, if you're reading this, remember that you never forbade us from self-defense.

I tried out my own form of passive resistance one night when a few of the other girls were keeping me awake. I was up at 5 a.m. thanks to my drunk-ass, noisy roommates, and to top it off, our house was disgusting. I mean, there was maple syrup on the goddamn phone! I couldn't take it anymore. So I pulled a couple of cookie sheets out of the kitchen cabinet and, well, started my own marching band.

"I CAN'T GET NO SLEEP CAUSE OF Y'ALL!" I screamed.

It's not like I was just running around blindly screaming my head off; my sense of rhythm is too good for that. The end result was actually pretty catchy.

I can't get no sleep cause of y'all!

You can't get no sleep cause of me!

I stormed around the house, yelling as loud as I possibly could. (Which is pretty damn loud.)

Go ahead, look it up on YouTube if you haven't seen it. I'm not embarrassed.

I was already known as a bit of a character on the show, but things kind of blew up after that episode aired. The "Get the Fuck Up" video went viral. Someone even made a remix! (He's no DJ Clue, but it's catchy enough.)

You never know what is going to set off momentum in your career, and you don't always have control over the opportunities that present themselves.

But when opportunity does knock, you better open that fucking door, let it in, and make it some brownies!

For me, strangely enough, a big break came in the form of a couple of cookie sheets and a 5 a.m. freak out. That's when people started to realize that I'm a whole lot more than just some one-off, crazy-ass bad girl.

I'm a crazy-ass bad girl who is funny, smart, and (gasp!) talented—and a woman who is committed to doing things her own way.

CHAPTER 4

The Godmother of All Bad Girls

So, what have we learned so far?

I can already see you typing up your online review:

"Tanisha Thomas gives bad advice. She condones cafeteria fist fights, showing up late to auditions [don't forget I was also sopping wet and angry!], and getting famous from a temper tantrum."

Well, better a temper tantrum than a sex tape, honey.

Here's the thing: sometimes the best you can do is, well... you. When I was filming *Bad Girls Club,* I was an immature, short-tempered twenty-one-year-old. But I wasn't afraid to just be Tanisha, flaws and all, on television, and people seemed to recognize that. So while it didn't always show me in the best light, Bad Girls Club opened a lot of doors for me and gave me a chance to prove myself.

When BGC aired, I started getting a lot of requests for interviews and other shows. Everything happened so quickly! I became known as "The Godmother of All Bad Girls," and the emails and messages poured in from fans around the world. This was the biggest, most wonderful surprise for me. I'm just Tanisha from Brooklyn, I kept thinking. How could all these strangers want to get to know me? But the most amazing people started reaching out to me, encouraging me and sharing their stories.

A lot of people equate fame with perfection. We see these A-list celebrities with banging bodies and flawless skin, and we put them high up on a pedestal.

Good for them.

That will never be me, though. You've all seen me at some of my worst moments, but I'm not ashamed because it's real. I'm not ashamed to let you peek behind the curtain, to see me in my nightgown with no makeup on, or to open up to you about my insecurities. I'd rather be authentic than perfect. I'll bare it all and keep it one hundred with you—because the truth is, none of us are perfect!

I've realized over the years that honesty is my biggest asset, and it's allowed me to connect and relate to fans. Listen, it's not easy to get up in front of the world and say, "Here I am. Sometimes I have it together, but sometimes I'm a hot mess." So many celebrities hide who they are for the sake of an image.

But I can't sugarcoat shit. I'll give you the real.

That's me: I'm a work in progress, and I'm not ashamed to put that out there. It's a more powerful message than you might think.

It's crazy to think that you're living your life and doing your thing, and you don't often stop to think about how your decisions might be affecting a stranger. This is true whether you're famous or not, but honestly, I didn't realize the impact I could have on others until I was on TV. I wasn't trying to help anybody—I was just being myself!

I get letters, emails, and Tweets from all different kinds of people. I hear from mothers who have plus sized daughters who have been bullied because of their weight, who are self-conscious and insecure, who feel better about themselves when they see me on TV. They tell me that my confidence gives them hope, that I provide a voice for them in mainstream media.

To the fans who have encouraged me: you guys have no idea how much your love and support means to me. I feel closer to some of you whom I've never met face to face than I do some family. I appreciate you all.

This is why I make it my duty to always be truthful on camera. Somewhere out there, I know that someone is struggling though the same issues that I am, and I want to be open and honest. It's my job, and I owe it to people.

Anyway, while I was riding high on my newfound popularity, VH1 offered me *Celebrity Fit Club.* I thought to myself, Tape another show and lose weight? This is a no brainer.

Celebrity Fit Club started out a little rough—I'll admit it, my attitude needed some work—but I ended up confronting a lot of the anger issues that are tied to my weight gain. In the end my team won and I lost twenty-four pounds.

It took me signing a contract with another network for Oxygen to realize they wanted to keep me around. (Networks can be just like men, did you know? They don't know what they got till it's gone. SMH.) But this time, they didn't want me to be a reality star. They wanted me to be a guest host on the BGC spin-off Love Games.

Now, it's one thing to be on a show like BGC and more or less have total freedom over what you do and say and not worry about how the episode will take shape. As a host, though, you not only need to be articulate, composed, and on your toes, you need to run shit. You need to react to and control what other people are doing. You need to play quarterback.

It's like they asked me to fill in for Eli Manning after spending a year chugging beers in the bleachers.

I don't usually back away from a challenge, but I was terrified. "I can't do it!" I told the producers. "I'm not a host, I'm the fucking Godmother of All Bad Girls." But they believed in me, and they encouraged me, so I accepted.

Well, all those improv lessons ended up being good for something. I wasn't just good at hosting, I enjoyed it! I've always had a knack for connecting with others. I can get the shiest person in the room to warm up to me and start spilling her juiciest secrets. It all comes in handy when I host. Hosting lets me channel all that Tanisha on steroids energy into something positive, playful, and fun. It brings out the best in me and keeps me away from the real drama. (And believe me, there was plenty of drama on Love Games.)

And lucky for me, it turned out that Oxygen wasn't just offering me a guest host gig, they were testing me to host the next season of Love Games.

So I took that test, and I passed. The next thing I knew, I had graduated from Bad Girl to Hostess with the Mostess.

CHAPTER 5

Controlled Chaos:
The BGC Reunions

Can you imagine how I felt hosting my first BGC reunion?

I'll break it down for you. There I was on stage in front of a live studio audience, sitting in a big, comfortable chair placed front and center. My hair and makeup was flawless, my wardrobe was on point, and I was flashing a huge smile for the camera.

I was thinking, *Holy Crap! This. Shit. Is. Fucking. Crazy.*

Here's the thing: hosting *any* television show is difficult. As a host, you're constantly struggling between following a script and reacting to what's happening live, right in front of your eyes. Even if every line is planned out for you in advance, there might be a moment where you have to say *fuck it,* throw that plan out the window and just go with the flow. You need to think before you act, you need to be on your toes at all times. It's exciting, but also *really* nerve wracking.

Now, hosting a BGC reunion is a whole different animal. No offense, Mr. Trebek, but this isn't some *Jeopardy!* shit. The Bad

Girls are about as unpredictable as it gets. These bitches are live wires, and they are very emotionally invested in what goes down at the reunion. Filming a whole season of BGC is hard: a lot of these girls can't handle the pressure cooker and are kicked out for fighting or leave voluntarily. Some of them stick through it and actually experience real personal growth, or just spend a full season doing the same crazy shit over and over again. Either way, this girls are almost always showing up to the reunion with serious baggage, hoping to resolve their unfinished beef—or, once in a while, to start some whole new beef. At the reunions, the Bad Girls know that their reputations are on the line, and that for some of them, this might be their last opportunity to speak their minds and set the story straight on television. The stakes are high.

If you watch the show, you know that the tension and the fighting are relentless. But there's so much drama off camera! Even if the girls don't want to see each other after filming stops, they often run into each other. They do a lot of appearances and club events, they form new cliques, and the drama continues on the social media front.

"She talked crap about me on Instagram," is not a phrase we threw around during Season Two but honey, times have changed! An all out war can break out with a simple tweet or subliminal post.

Seriously, with the fighting that happens on that damn stage, sometimes I think I should be on stage in hockey gear. Helmet, facemask, pads—the works!! At least, I should have a back-up weave for all the hair pulling that goes on.

So when the producers first offered me the hosting job, I thought, they couldn't possibly be serious. I didn't think I could handle the responsibility. Not only would I have to run the show, I'd be acting as the face of a network. I would have a lot to lose. And "think before you act" hadn't been in my vocabulary up to that point. As a former Bad Girl, I was worried I'd get caught up in the drama and throw a punch or two.

Here's an important tip for TV hosts: don't punch your guests. (Even if they deserve it.)

I won't lie, though: I love a challenge. I was nervous about hosting, but I'm a go-getter and I know that I can do whatever I put my mind to. I'm also a perfectionist. I'm a Virgo, remember? So not only was I determined to step up to the plate, I decided I would be the best damn host out there. Even if I didn't get it right at first, I was going to work until I made it right.

Nothing could prepare me for that shit, though!

Here's what hosting a BGC reunion is actually like:

I get a script a few days in advance. I study it until I know it by heart.

Three hours before we start filming, that script gets thrown out. They hand me a new one while I'm in hair and makeup. At this point, all I want to do is relax, take a deep breath, and gear myself up for a long, unpredictable day of filming. But instead I'm frantically reading the new script, trying to memorize my lines, while my face is getting beat and my hair is getting tugged on.

Whether I know the script or not, when I step out on stage, it's go time. I shouldn't feel alone out there: I have a cold open more or less memorized, I have a teleprompter in front of me with some generic guidelines, and I wear an ear bud so the producers can talk me through the curve balls that that these bitches will undoubtedly throw my way. It's a well designed support system to keep things on track.

Piece of cake, right?

But then the first fight breaks out, the ear bud falls out, the teleprompter goes down, everyone's looking at me, and I have to have my shit together.

This one is crying. OK, let her cry.

These two are about to fight. Get out of the fucking way!

Get those two to stop screaming over each other so we can understand what they're saying.

Stay calm, stay genuine, keep the flow going.

More crying. I need a margarita.

Lots of cursing. Let's hope the censors catch all of that.

Here come the claws! Duck!

Shit is going haywire. Time to EXIT STAGE RIGHT!!

The first reunion I hosted was Season Eight: Las Vegas. As it turns out, throwing a bunch of Bad Girls together in Sin City creates a lot of chaos. Shocking, I know. That season started with seven girls, but it played out like a game of musical chairs. Bitches got kicked out, clawed out, shoved out. The five that came to the reunion were the last women standing—and each one had a score to settle.

I'll never forget stepping out on that stage for the first time. I felt that rush of energy that I've been chasing ever since my high school performances, that feeling of adrenaline that comes from having all eyes on me and knowing that I'm in control of the room.

"What's up everybody?" I said. "It's about to go down!"

It certainly was about to go down.

By the end of taping for part one of the reunion, shit was popping off. Three of the girls got really heated. They started screaming and things turned physical. I tried to intervene and keep them talking, but I couldn't get a damn word in! So I gave up. I sat back, ate some popcorn and watched the catfight unfold. Eventually I had to run for cover. (Can you imagine me running? It's pretty crazy.)

I told you, this is not some *Jeopardy!* shit.

Even when the reunions turn into total pandemonium, they usually end up being cathartic for most of the girls. Some of them will never be friends. But clearing the air tends to help, and I like getting them together one last time and giving them a forum for speaking their minds.

And don't get me wrong: I've been running my mouth about how crazy these damn reunions are, but I'm so grateful to have the opportunity to host. Grateful for my management, and for the people at Oxygen who saw the potential in me, who realized that there's more to me than a crazy mouth and a short temper. They took a chance on me, and it paid off. For that I am so thankful.

The reunions are intense, though, and the process is very draining. Taping for each reunion takes between twelve and thirteen hours. After a full day I'm DONE. I'm not just physically exhausted, I'm emotionally wrung out. I've actually sat in my dressing room and cried after a few reunions.

Because here's the thing: these are real people.

You're thinking, *I know that. Of course they're real people.* But we forget that all the time! We see reality stars getting in fights and acting crazy and we assume it is all fake, that they are just doing it for our entertainment. We lose sight of the fact that we're watching their actual lives.

I see some of these girls' faces and they look like deer in headlights. I know what they're thinking: *Is this my life? How did I get to this point?*

I feel for them because I've been there. The thing is, when you go on *Bad Girls Club* and act like a crazy bitch it feels normal. It's how you got on the show in the first place and it's what you signed up for. Popping off, starting shit, pulling hair: it all feels like the right thing to do because everyone is acting that way and egging you on. But something happens when you go home and watch yourself on television. You see these moments that make you think, "Oh my God, who is that? I shouldn't have done that, I shouldn't have said that."

It's a big an a-ha moment, and you realize that you need to change. You realize that life is just so much bigger than just fighting, cursing, and just being bad. There's so much more out there, so many ways to live to your fullest potential. These girls need to realize that they can do so much more with the opportunities they've been given.

I know what they're going through. It helps me to be a better host—and a better friend. And it's part of my job as the Godmother of Bad Girls. I'm the peacemaker, the Fairy Godmother, and the Mama Bear. It means I get pulled into a lot of the drama, but I honestly don't mind. I know that, even though the girls act tough, sometimes they just need a sister. They need someone to listen and a shoulder to cry on.

I love what I do. I truly believe that God has placed me exactly where he needs to be. I laugh and play along but I keep it one hundred with the girls. I love these women like they're my sisters, and sometimes a bit of tough love goes a long way.

The Bad Girls need to realize that all unnecessary fighting and cliques don't help them. A lot of these girls have had tough lives, and if they recognized that it's them against the world instead of them against each other, they'd be a lot better off.

Don't get me wrong: I love natural drama. Do some bitches deserve to get punched in the face? Absolutely. People like to see a train wreck, but it gets to a point where it's not funny anymore.

The trick is to figure out who needs to get punched in the face—and who needs help. And the ultimate lesson of all is not every thing requires a reaction. Sometimes silence is the best answer for a fool.

CHAPTER 6

"Larger Than Life" Is A Euphemism

I asserted my self-confidence on day one of Bad Girls Club. "I am P.H.A.T.," I announced on national television. "Pretty hot, and so damn thick."

Look up a group photo of the cast of Season Two and you'll understand why I felt the need to say that. I was the heaviest girl on the show by far, and my choices were to either project strength, confidence, and a kick ass personality, or be known as the insecure fat girl in a sea of little Barbies.

When I did *Celebrity Fit Club* I lost a dramatic amount of weight. But when the show ended I started yo-yo-ing. I had a hard time sticking to the diet and exercise routine. My weight has been up and down, and it's been hard.

But I'm not embarrassed! There are millions and millions of Americans struggling with their weight. I'm not alone.

Ladies, I've said it before and I'll say it again: get to know your worth, know what you have, and no one can ever take that from you.

I haven't always felt this way. When I was younger, I struggled with low self-esteem at times. And the funny thing is I was so much smaller then! My mom has never been a fan of me being a big girl. She's very superficial, and in her eyes, big was not a good thing unless it was cold hard cash.

"You don't need to eat that, Tanisha," she'll say, or, "You need to wear stronger shapewear."

It's tough to hear that from your own mom, the person who should make you feel good about yourself, no matter what.

It took me a while to get to the point where her words wouldn't bother me, but now I just don't care. "OK, Ma, whatever," I say, humoring her. For a long time I questioned her methods but in a way I think she's done me a favor.

As it turns out years of her ridicule prepared me for the harsh feedback from the public. Try being an overweight reality TV star, and you'll wish you had a mama that gave you a thick skin.

It's hard being a plus sized woman in the entertainment industry. Being a plus sized actress is tough enough: I've gone to LA for jobs where the casting team would automatically state what dress size the actresses needed to be on the audition sheet. Guess how many times that's worked out for me?

Right, zero fucking times.

With reality TV, though, it's even harder. Reality TV stars are not only judged by the industry, we're picked apart by the audience, week after week. You represent yourself on reality TV, you're not just playing a role. If you say something that people don't like, they're coming for you.

And the first thing that they love to pick on is your weight.

I know what you're thinking, honey. This is all part of being on television. And the thing is, I'm so grateful for every opportunity that I've been given. It's a one in a million chance to be able to be on TV doing what I love.

But I'll be honest: it's stressful. Sometimes I think there is no freedom of speech in the public eye. Everyone nitpicks everything you say. t frustrating to have people you've never even met—never even talked to!—tear you to pieces on Twitter, Instagram or on some blog, but you know what? It just reflects badly on them. There are people out there who are so insecure that it's a shame. Insecurity is an ugly trait. It makes you hate people you don't even know.

To the haters: don't confuse entertainment and real life. We have got to stop the negativity. It's one thing to offer constructive criticism, it's another to be a flat out hater over someone you don't even know. It really does say a lot about how you truly feel about yourself. There's so much negativity and hate out there, it's honestly disgusting. You think it makes you superior and stronger than the rest of us, but when I read your comments all I see is a bunch of miserable, unhappy, self-hating bitches. Make sure everything is in order and those hands are squeaky clean before you go pointing those fingers!

We need to stick together! What would happen if we tried to be a little nicer, a little more helpful? To—God forbid—give someone the benefit of the doubt before you judge them? You'd be surprised by what simple acts of kindness can do for someone else and for you.

If only those people could focus all that negative energy into something positive, the world be a much better place.

Try as you might, you can't please everybody. You have to be yourself, and ultimately I decided I'm just going to do what I'm going to do, ME!

Over time, I've learned to let the comments about my weight roll off my back. Someone calls me fat and I say, "What else you got?"

I can lose weight, you can't lose that ugliness.

And to all my plus sized ladies out there, you know that you don't have to be on television to struggle with this shit. It's hard to date when you're overweight. Men feel like they're doing you a favor! They assume you're going to be a sugar momma, or that you're desperate. Well, listen up: Fellas you better rewind and come again, honey, because that shit isn't flying over here!

I hear from women all the time that their boyfriends are upset because they've gained weight. But the real problem is that these women don't love themselves. If you look in the mirror and you don't like what's looking back at you, by all means, fix it. Fix it so that you—not anybody else—likes what you see in the mirror. If you don't love yourself then you'll always be going after people who don't love you. Only you hold the key to your happiness. No one else.

Unfortunately, we live in a society where the entertainment industry really defines our culture. It defines what's beautiful, what's hot, what's not. This girl with long, sleek hair is beautiful, this exotic girl is beautiful, the one who's taken a rib out, this one with the photoshopped twenty-inch waist and the big booty. It's not realistic, and it's not attainable.

Five Things People Need to STOP Doing to Big Girls:

*   Assuming that we are loud, angry, and intimidating. Listen, I know I'm intimidating, but it has nothing to do with my dress size. Honey, I'd be loud even if I was a double zero.
*   This one is for the men: Thinking that a food is the way to our hearts. I've seen it all, from "let me make you a nice dinner" to "I'd like to hit it from the back while you eat a piece of fried chicken." WTF! You think you can just drop some food and I'll come running? Talk to my doctor: I'm supposed to be on a liquid diet anyway.
*   Calling us cute (Kittens are cute! I'm a grown ass woman!) or complimenting our pretty faces, just to avoid commenting on our bodies.
*   Hooking us up with your fat friends. I like my men big, but just because we're both chubby doesn't mean we have a single thing in common.
*   Providing commentary on everything we eat. If I'm enjoying a damn salad, I'm not necessarily on a diet. If I'm eating a cupcake, JUST LET ME LIVE!!

Five Things Big Girls Need to STOP Doing to Themselves:

*   Skipping the shapewear. Say it with me now: "Spanx is my friend."

- Wearing the wrong size. Just face facts: you might need to go up a size or two, but your clothes will look much better on you.
- Looking to supermodels and photoshopped magazine covers to motivate you to lose weight. Open your eyes— 99.99% of real women don't look like that!
- Hating their bodies. Think of your body as your friend. You need to love and honor your curves! Look at yourself in the mirror every morning and tell yourself that you are beautiful. You will be amazed by how effective this is.
- Dating men who hate their bodies. Life is too short to waste your time with someone who doesn't love you for who you are.

Of course, loving your body is easier said than done. If you're a plus sized fashionista like me, you know how hard it can be to find clothes that look good and actually fit you. This is why my best friend Bella and I got together to launch Plush, a custom clothing line for curvy and fabulous women. We want women to embrace who they are, love who they are, and just let their light shine. It's not just a fashion line, it's a movement: be bold, be you, be yourself.

Ladies, we can define what beautiful is. Let me tell you, I have been approached by so many diets and doctors for endorsements, and I've turned them all down. As I get older, I recognize the need to lose weight. If I lose fifty pounds it'll save me from a lot of trouble down the road. I'll be healthier, I'll be more comfortable, I'll be able to chase a cute boy down the street and ask for his number. But it's important to me to stay true to myself because I have a platform where I can speak up about loving the skin you're in.

I want to be healthy. Do I need to be a stick figure and fit into what society says is normal? Absolutely not.

Why be normal when you can be fabulous?

CHAPTER 7

The Devil Doesn't Only Wear Prada

I'm not only obsessed with food and hot guys; I also have a passion for fashion. There's just something about a well-dressed woman that inspires everyone. My mother always told me that a woman dressed to kill could take over the entire world!

Now, although I love fashion, like a lot of things in my life it doesn't exactly love me back...

One summer while filming a new show in L.A., I discovered a beautiful, grand outdoor mall located directly across from my new swanky apartment. I mean, what could be better? I lived in one of the most sought after apartment buildings in the neighborhood, every day was a guaranteed sunny day, and L.A. is home to some of the most elaborate and glamorous shopping malls known to man.

I was bursting with excitement as I skipped across to the Nordstrom entrance. Once inside I could barely keep my composure! The designer bags, the fine jewelry and, *oh my God,*

THE SHOES! I was surrounded by sparkling, perfectly organized merchandise that I swear was just begging to come home with me.

Normally I know better than to ever step foot on the clothing floor. Especially at a place like this. I mean you'd be lucky if a dress came in a large! And if there's one thing I hate to do it's just stand by staring at an item and thinking, *damn, I wish it would fit me.* But this time I couldn't help it. The layout of the selling floor got me. So before you know it I started to whisk my way through the perfectly tailored floor and attempted to shop.

And then it happened.

I came face to face with the most beautiful dress I had ever laid eyes on: a red lace layered A-line Ted Baker creation that seemed absolutely perfect for me.

Except there was one teeny little problem…they only went up to a size twelve.

Now, I've been down this road before, and usually at this point I just curse under my breath and console myself with a new purse or shoes. But THIS time I was determined! I just had to figure out a way to try this dress on. Even if it didn't close I just wanted to envision what it could potentially look like. So I grabbed the biggest size off the rack and headed over to the fitting room.

Now I don't know if all big girls go through this, but I hate— and I mean HATE—trying things on! I want to feel like it's a private moment, but you never really feel alone in there. It's like everyone is waiting for an impromptu fashion show. I try to combat this by always like trying on things alone. And by alone I mean no friends, no guys—*no one* in the fitting room wanting to "see."

I'm here to try on clothes, not be a spectacle!

So imagine my anxiety when I was greeted by the fitting room attendant. "Oh, that's a hot little number you got there," she said. "These just came in and everyone loves them—they are flying off the rack."

All I could do was smile trying to hide some of me behind the dress. I couldn't help feeling awkward, but I walked into the dressing room and proceeded to try on the most beautiful dress in the world. I unzipped the back as far down as it would go, then I stepped into it and tried my best to work my arms through the sleeves. Done. Then I carefully pulled it up, ever so slowly, so it was right on my shoulders and cautiously handled the lace... At this point I was sweating buckets and somewhat out of breath but I had to get that zipper closed.

I'm not delusional: I knew the dress wasn't going to fit. If it had been any other dress I would have stopped, made some excuse to the attendant as to why I didn't need the dress, and bounced.

But nope, had to have this one zipped.

So I undid the arms, turned the dress around, sucked in my gut really, *really* tight and pulled the zipper as far as it would go. Then I placed my hands back inside and just when I was about to pop my new dress dance—the zipper *popped off!*

The damn thing busted open with such force I felt like a can of Grands Biscuits!

Starting to panic. I reached back to grab the zipper off the floor.

Then I heard a loud rip from under the arms.

I was mortified. There I was in this $500 dress and I had turned myself into Shrek trying to put it on.

SMH.

I ended up leaving the dress in the dressing room and easing out of the store like a fugitive. I was so paranoid that someone witnessed the whole thing I just had to get out of there.

Learned my lesson that day: designer dressers are fucking evil!

The devil doesn't only wear Prada, honey—he wears Ted Baker, too.

CHAPTER 8

The Groupie Life

You know me as loud, no-holds-barred Tanisha, but do you want to see me get shy and timid real quick?

Just give me a tour of Shaq's house while my friend is upstairs getting a private tour of his...um, bedroom.

OK, OK, I'm getting ahead of myself. I'll back up a bit. A few years ago I flew out to L.A. to film a pilot. This is one thing most people don't know about me: I've filmed a lot of pilots. The process of getting a TV show on air is lengthy and uncertain, and ultimately only about a quarter of pilots end up becoming series.

Anyway, this particular trip to L.A. was for my own "reality" show. I'm putting quotes around the word because there wasn't much that was real about it. The show was supposed to be about my life, except it was set in L.A. in an apartment they'd rented out for me, and my co-stars were a bunch of women they'd cast to be my friends.

I was so confused. Here I was, this raw, honest, hilarious girl with an outsized personality, and all of a sudden I was pretending to be best friends with a bunch of girls who should have been on

The Hills. Don't get me wrong: my real friends come from all different backgrounds, walks of life, and races. It's not as if I only associate with people who look like me and talk like me. But these girls! These were people I would never associate with.

Here's the thing: as a reality TV star, you have to be really careful. You want to keep working and making money and keeping up your profile, and it's always exciting when a new opportunity comes along. You never want to turn down projects. But sometimes it just doesn't feel right.

That was the case with this show (and is probably why it never made it beyond the pilot, by the way). It just wasn't my story. I knew this from day one, and I was stressed out throughout the entire process. On our last night of taping we filmed at a restaurant, and I was in such a rush to leave production. I just had to get away. So when I found out that Soulja Boy was throwing a party at a club in Beverly Hills that night, I fled the scene.

I took a cab to the club and it was buzzing. The paparazzi were swarming the place, and there were groupies everywhere.

And—surprise, surprise—I ran into the biggest groupie I know.

If I use this girl's real name she'll sue me, so I'll call her Melody. ("Melody," if you read this, be a friend and don't sue me). Like me, Melody was a former Bad Girl who maintained her own type of notoriety long after her season ended. We had a very tumultuous relationship over the years: one minute we loved each other and the next minute we'd be at each other's throats. And none of this was my fault. Each and every time I've told myself I'm done with her, Melody has found a way to trick me, to make me think that she is an honest, reliable person, and then I'd forgive her and fall into her trap. Rinse and repeat.

Melody and I were on the downswing the night we bumped into each other at the club—we were definitely not on the best terms at the time—but we were both happy to see a familiar face and latched onto each other as we entered the party. And I'm not kidding when I say that all eyes were on her when we walked through the door. This girl was in a painted on white dress that fit her like a glove. Her curves were in all the right places, and the guys couldn't stop staring. Soulja Boy walked in with his entourage and spotted Melody immediately, so before I knew it, we were sitting with him in the VIP section! The music was pumping, the drinks were flowing—it was unbelievable.

After an hour or so we left Soulja Boy's party and went to Trousdale in North Hollywood. We skipped the ridiculously long line, Melody cursing out TMZ as we walked by (this girl was always hoping to end up on some viral video, with no such luck). I had thought that Soulja Boy's party was star-studded, but Trousdale was filled with celebrities. I spotted Lindsay Lohan and couldn't fight the urge to ask for a selfie.

"Hi Lindsay, do you mind if…" Then I thought better of it. She looked like she was just trying to have fun—I couldn't blame her.

My parents used to tell me not to tag along with the friends that they knew were a bad influence. Don't follow So-and-So, they'd say. She'll just lead you astray.

Well, Melody was definitely one of the friends they would warn me about. It was one of the most exciting nights of my life, though. I wasn't drunk or on drugs—it was just the thrill of it all.

Melody and I left the club around 2 a.m. with a bunch of celebs and groupies. We ended up in two different cars and got chased by the paparazzi. It was crazy! And to top it off, we ended up at Leonardo DiCaprio's house! I had no idea when we pulled into the driveway—we just walked in the door and I was in complete shock. He had one of the most amazing houses I'd ever seen in my entire life. I couldn't believe it: I had spent the night rubbing shoulders with celebrities and there I was at Leo's house!

Now on top of Leo being drop dead gorgeous, so was his home! A beautiful massive mansion located in Beverly Hills that was fit for a king, there was a fish tank from the floor to the ceiling, an out of this world custom gourmet kitchen! A living and dining room that was beautifully decorated and inviting, and a movie screening room that was out of this world!

Does this all seem kind of unbelievable? I know. What I realized really quickly during my time in L.A., though, is that when it comes to celebrity culture it is completely different from New York. On the east coast I've bumped into a few celebrities at events or at high-end stores, but for the most part they do their own thing—it's very hush hush and secret. In L.A., however, celebrities seem to hang out in an open circle, including reality stars, groupies. It's way more laid back. If they like you, you're in.

And everyone seemed to like Melody that night. She tried her luck with Leo, but he hooked up with Meagan Good instead.

Melody started talking to some other people and tried to take me to another party at 4 a.m., but it fell through. That was fine by me. I was tired, and I'd had about enough excitement for a lifetime.

But don't worry—I'll get to Shaq!

The next day, Melody met up for breakfast in Santa Monica to rehash our incredible evening.

"Girl, I had an amazing time," I told her as I took my seat in the restaurant. "No one will believe that happened!"

"Tanisha, I have something to tell you," she said, looking like the cat who got the cream. "Do you remember those guys I was talking to at the end of the night?"

Between you and me, Melody had talked to a lot of guys that night, so I wasn't sure.

"Well," she continued. "Some of them were basketball players. I've gone to a couple of games, and Shaq wants to take me out."

Before I had a chance to pick my jaw up off the floor, her phone rang.

AS GOD IS MY WITNESS, IT WAS SHAQ.

Melody played it pretty cool, but I was freaking the fuck out! I could hear him on the phone.

"What are you up to?" he asked.

"I'm having brunch with Tanisha," she said.

I kicked her hard under the table. "Shh! Don't tell him it's me!" I whispered as quietly as I could (which is not that quietly).

"Come to Bel-Air," he said. "Bring your friend."

For the first time in my entire life, I didn't finish my meal. I was a wreck. My heart was so beating so fast I thought it was going to burst out of my chest. Normally I don't get that star struck.

But this was SHAQ! I'd grown up watching him play basketball. He'd been one of the most famous NBA players in the world for most of my lifetime…and now we were going to his house. So my friend could have sex with him.

As nervous as I was, I didn't dare say I wasn't going. So Melody and I paid our bill, touched up our makeup in the bathroom, and headed out to Shaq's house.

Finding Shaq's house was another story. We pulled into his neighborhood and all we saw were luxury cars lining the curbs. I'm not kidding: there was not one car not from that year. We knew we had the right street, but we could not find the damn house! As it turned out, it was a brand new house and he'd just moved in—this was not long after he and his ex-wife Shaunie split up—so the GPS could not pick up the address.

There we were, driving around Bel-Air with our mouths hanging open, staring at the enormous houses. Then Melody's phone rang.

Once again, it was Shaq.

"Is that you in the white BMW truck?" he asked.

"Yeah, that's me," Melody said.

My already racing heart kicked up a notch. Is Shaq spying on us? Does he have cameras all over the neighborhood?

"I told you," he continued. "You were supposed to call me when you got to the intersection and my driver will take you in."

Sure enough, two seconds later a black Mercedes pulled up next to us, and Shaq's driver motioned for us to follow.

I'm telling you, I think it's easier to invade Fort Knox than get to Shaq's front door.

Anyway, we pulled through the gates and, honey, I heard angels sing and doves fly. I got out of the car and felt like I was going to faint. There I was on the front steps of Shaq's mansion. It was so far away from where I grew up, something that I could only dream of when I was a little girl. It was insane.

We walked inside and Melody started strutting around like she was accustomed to the place. I, on the other hand, was terrified. We heard heavy (seven foot!) footsteps coming down the stairs and I grabbed Melody's arm.

"He's coming!" I whispered frantically. "What am I going to do?"

"Tanisha," she snapped. "Play it cool, OK?"

All I could do was stare at the floor. He introduced himself and I finally looked up, blushing and sweating like a crazy person. He's just huge in person—it's very intimidating. I tried my best to keep my cool, though, and we all chatted for a minute and before he invited Melody upstairs.

"I'll be back in a bit," she said—and then she left me all alone in the kitchen! What would you do if you were left alone in Shaq's mansion?

The first thing I did was peek into the fridge. I just wanted to know what the man eats. And it was bizarre! There was no plethora of things to choose from: just pre-made meals in black containers with clear lids, organized to a T. His personal chef must have OCD. I spotted some sparkling water, but there was no fruit punch (!), and no snacks. Shaq, where are the snacks when you need them?

I closed the refrigerator door and started taking pictures on my phone. I spotted a painting in the corner and turned to snap a picture when I had a weird feeling that someone was watching me. I whipped around and there was this tall guy standing behind me (no, not as tall as Shaq).

"Oh hi, I didn't see you," I said, trying to play it cool.

He started walking toward me and I was convinced that I was in trouble, that I was about to get kicked out.

"I'll give you a tour," he said calmly.

Phew.

"That's OK—I'm just waiting for my friend," I replied.

"She'll be a while," he said with a smirk.

So I agreed to the tour. And of course the house was beautiful, with an amazing infinity pool built into a cliff so high up above the city that I was scared to approach it. While we walked around the first floor, Shaq's friend said what every wingman says to the unhappy girl who's left over: "Why are you so quiet? You're being a little antisocial."

I was about to explain to him that I'm never antisocial—and then I realized he was flirting with me. Birds of a feather flock together, I thought to myself. He thought something was going to go down!

And the thing is, I'm usually one to grab life by the horns, especially when it comes to men. I'm not shy, and I'm rarely intimidated in these kinds of situations. But I really clammed up that afternoon. I was cautious. Not only was I completely overwhelmed by Shaq's house and the excess of his house, there was something really off about the situation. My tour guide had clearly been in this situation before—maybe hundreds of times, who knows!—and I kept wondering how many women Shaq had at his beck and call.

The man could do this all day! A woman every hour. Why not?

Thankfully, just when I started getting really uncomfortable, Melody called me upstairs. I was so relieved—until I went up and found her walking around the bedroom stark naked, with Shaq talking like nothing was going on! He told us to bring our friends back the next day for a house party and that he wanted to hook me up with his brother, but I had to fly back to New York the following morning (thankfully so—because I don't know what would have happened!).

Shaq seemed like a nice enough guy, but his life is unreal. I've told this story to so many people who aren't at all surprised. He's been doing it for years, they tell me. He has dozens of side chicks, he takes care of his girls, he gives them money, he's never faithful to his girlfriends.

I mean, one week after Melody hooked up with Shaq, we found out that he had proposed to his girlfriend, Hoopz. I'm sure this story wouldn't surprise her all that much.

I used to think that dating a professional athlete would really be the life. A hot man in my bed, financial security, an enormous house, etc., etc. I used to think that money would alleviate your personal problems, and that at the end of the day, it would trump all.

But if money is the key to happiness, then why are so many rich people so dysfunctional? Why do so many celebrities die so young?

And these athletes that have so much money and so many options…as a wife or a girlfriend, how could I deal with that shit? How can you expect your man to be faithful when he can call up a hundred different women and have them in his bed within the hour?

Life's too short for that kind of aggravation. So I decided right then and there that I would never be with a man just for the money and the lifestyle.

To be honest, sometimes I think I was happier when I was a retail manager than I've been as a reality TV superstar. My life was simpler, I had realer and stronger friendships, I had less weight on my shoulders and fewer people around me with their hands out. It's amazing how much people ask from you when they think you're doing well for yourself.

But that's OK. I know how to deal with it. And as for my twenty-four hours of living the groupie life, no harm done. At least I got a tour of Shaq's house out of the experience.

CHAPTER 9

MÉNAGE À TROIS

Let's check in on how closely you've been paying attention. Remember Chapter 1, when my father uttered those ominous words as he swept up the remains of my piggy bank?

Men are going to be the death of my little girl. I just know it.

Well, Daddy could have made a living as the Brooklyn Medium, because he saw the future right then and there. I am cursed.

It's bad enough that my jeans don't fit. It's bad enough that I have to double—even triple—up on the Spanx. When it comes to men, I just can't call it. I have no luck. I'm successful and confident in so many areas of my life, but for some reason I can't seem to find the right guy. Night after night, I have no one to come home to, no one to hold me, or make me a midnight snack.

When it comes to men, nothing fazes me. I've seen it all, I've had it all. I've left it all behind. My love life is so crazy that I've convinced myself that I have the starring role in a Lifetime movie. That thought—and a lot of red wine—gets me through all the drama.

Let me tell you about the first time I realized that the curse was real.

It all starts with some oxtail and rice.

Before I was cast on BGC I worked as a nurse's aide for the state of New York. I had an elderly patient who lived in Crown Heights, (my soon to be mother-in-law, but we'll get to that later) Brooklyn and loved her some Jamaican food. She was always asking me to go out to the local Jamaican restaurant, 3-D's, and pick up lunch for her. With all the health problems my patient had, I knew Jamaican food was the last thing she should be eating, but it made her happy and so every now and then, I would give in and get her some oxtail or curry goat with rice.

I'll be honest: my reluctance to go to 3-D's wasn't just about my patient's health. I tried to avoid that place because the chef would always hit on me. Now, I've been through a few relationships with Jamaican men. I used to be into them, but then I realized that there was a pattern when it came to these dudes. Jamaican men love women. I mean, most men love women, but when it comes to Jamaicans there is something kind of extra going on. I mean, they write songs about how much these guys love women. They can't get enough of us—which isn't always a good thing.

So when it came to Beres, the chef at 3-D's, I tried to keep my distance. He was alright-looking, but a bit on the older side. He wore a big flashy gold chain every day, and he shamelessly flirted with me. He was not shy: he'd straight up ask me out every time I walked in that door.

"Hi, can I have the oxtail please?"

"Girl, when am I going to take you out?"

"..."

This dude thinks he's twenty-one, I thought to myself. *I might need to choke him with that gold chain.*

After a few months of stopping by 3-D's and turning down Beres, I eventually caved. I was single with no romantic prospects—who was I to say no to a free meal, anyway? At least he was attractive and had a steady job. So I agreed to go to dinner with him, and you know what? We had a good time. We ate at a nice restaurant and he tried to go home with me, but I was determined to have him take me on a few dates before I let him get in my pants.

Beres and I were still talking and getting ready to see each other again when my friend Shakara called me up on a Saturday to ask if I wanted to go clubbing with her. I was partying pretty heavy in those days, and I never turned down a chance to go out with Shakara. She was also Jamaican—there's a theme in this story—and, like most good island girls, she was a party fanatic. In fact, we first met at a club: she was arguing with one bouncer because she'd forgotten her ID and couldn't get in, and I was arguing with the other bouncer because I didn't want to pay the $20 cover. (Ladies, none of you should ever pay a cover—ever.) Shakara and I clicked immediately, got into the club after some heated arguing, and the rest was history.

Anyway, I got all dolled up that night for our ladies' night. At the time I used to wear glasses, but of course they didn't go with my fly look, so I left them at home. I figured that, with or without my glasses, my vision would end up blurry by the end of the night.

When Shakara came to pick me up at my house, a man was driving her car. I got in the backseat behind him, so I didn't get a good look at his face—not that I could see too well without my glasses, anyway. The music was turned up loud in the car and neither of them said much during the short drive from my house to the club. We pulled up to the entrance, he gave her some money, and she leaned forward to kiss him goodbye. Mystery dude pulled back and Shakara slapped him playfully on the hand.

"Baby, don't be so shy," she said, kissing him on the mouth.

I didn't think much of it. I did, however, notice the wide grin on her face as we walked into the club.

"Girl, look at you," I said, grabbing her hand as we headed to the bar. "You're glowing!"

"It's my new boyfriend," she admitted, beaming. "We've been going out for a few months and he's so good to me. I think it's getting serious."

"Good for you!" I said. "You know, I actually met a guy recently that I really like. He's a bit older, but I'm OK with it."

"My man is older too!"

Hm. That's a coincidence.

"So where did you two meet?" I asked.

"Well, we met at the hospital where we both work. He has two jobs though—he's also a chef at a Jamaican restaurant."

Uh oh. "What restaurant?"

"I don't know the name," she replied. "I've never been there. But it's in Crown Heights."

No no no no no no. "Wait a minute," I said. "He's Jamaican and he works in Crown Heights? Is he light-skinned?"

She looked at me like I was a little crazy. "Tanisha, you just saw him in the car."

"I'm not wearing my glasses!" I said, starting to panic a little. "They didn't go with my look! And I sat behind him the whole time."

"Girl, why are you acting so weird?"

She's right, you're being crazy, I told myself. *It can't be the same guy.* "I'm sorry. Listen, all that matters is that you're happy."

She smiled. "I am. I'm so happy with Beres!"

Dammit! "BERES, THAT WORKS AT 3-D'S?"

"Um, yes . . . ?"

"Honey, we're dating the same guy."

Ladies night suddenly got a little awkward.

I tried to smooth things over. "Listen," I told Shakara. "It looks like you two have something more concrete going on."

"Yeah."

"I'll back off. You can have him."

I was hoping that would be the end of the world's most awkward *ménage à trois*.

Unfortunately, it was just the beginning.

Shakara went home that night and confronted Beres. He fed her a bunch of lies! *It's not like that, I didn't know you were friends*, the whole nine yards. He said when he saw me come out of my apartment building that night he almost threw up! That's why he hardly said a word in the car, that's why he reluctantly kissed her. (Despite everything, picturing about him sweating and trying not to puke while he drove us to the club still makes me laugh. Pimpin' ain't easy!)

But sure enough, within a day or two that motherfucker called me up and fed me a bunch of lies too!

"Tanisha, you're the one I want to be with," he said. "I think we have something going; I was about to go out and buy you some jewelry."

I did what a good friend should do: I cut him off, hung up, and called Shakara. I told her everything. At this point all I wanted to do was get her to leave this cheating son of a bitch, but she was convinced that I called him to try and win him back.

"You said you'd back off!" she yelled. Then it got even worse: she called him up on a three-way call and asked him who he wanted to be with.

"Tanisha?!" he said, incredulous, with no idea that I was listening. "I don't even know that girl. I don't want to be with her."

Huh.

Then it got worse.

"Baby, you're the one I want to be with," he continued. "You're the one with the nice sexy body. Why would I want her when I can have you?"

He went on and on. Um, hello? There he was, talking about me like I was a damn dog, and I was ON THE PHONE LISTENING.

I couldn't keep my mouth shut.

"You've got to be fucking kidding me!" I said, finally. "I have never been ugly one day in my life. I have never begged a man to be with me."

SMH.

I was already done with Beres, but this more or less ruined my friendship with Shakara. A lot of our friends—including me, of course—tried to convince her not to keep talking to him, but she didn't listen. In fact, as I'm writing this, she's still with him! And he's a great provider, I guess. He pays for everything, he treats her well, but as far as I'm concerned he is not to be trusted.

Shakara and I eventually drifted apart, which is fine by me. I can't remember the last time I spoke to her. It all works out the way it's supposed to, anyhow.

My oxtail-loving patient, however, still wanted her Jamaican fix on the regular. I tried my best to avoid it.

"Tanisha," she'd say. "Here's ten dollars. Can you go pick me something up at 3-D's?"

"Don't you want something else? Mexican? Chinese? How about I cook you something?" I pleaded. She refused. She damn near threw her shoe at me!

So eventually I gave in. I dragged my ass to the restaurant, and there was Beres, gold chain and all. As soon as I walked through the door he flashed me one of his big cheesy smiles.

I wasn't having it. "I'm only here because my patient insisted," I said.

"You don't have to worry." He kept grinning.

Turns out I did have to worry. There were two other people getting takeout in line behind me, and he took his damn time with my order, serving them first so that we could be alone. As soon as they left he tried to grab my hand over the counter.

"Beres," I said, pulling away. "You already said what you have to say."

"Baby, I was under so much pressure," he replied. "You don't understand."

He wouldn't let me pay for the food. I tried to take it and leave, but he came out from behind the counter to hand me the bag. I reached for it and he leaned over to grab me.

I didn't hesitate.

I ripped the bag of food out of his hands and kicked that motherfucker right in the balls.

"You're a piece of shit!" I yelled, and stormed out.

"I'm so sorry, I can't go back to 3-D's," I told my patient as I handed her the container of oxtail. "The guy there is really rude and I just can't stand him."

I waited for her to fling her shoe.

"Oh, honey, that's fine," she said. "You can just go to the other location."

Yes, that's right: there was another location the whole time!

If only I had known that—I would have saved myself a boatload of trouble!

CHAPTER 10

Tanisha Gets Divorced
(Well, She Tries To)

Prince Charming will come find you one day, just you wait.
When you find Mr. Right, he'll take care of you for the rest of
your life.
Wait for the right guy—he's out there!

This is the kind of terrible advice I've been getting from my parents since I was twelve years old. When I was growing up they had me convinced that there was a perfect man out there, waiting around with a bouquet of long stemmed roses just for me.

I can't even write that sentence without rolling my eyes.

I can't fault them too much for their delusions: they're both Caribbean, both very traditional, and they came to the United States expecting to make a better life—and give me an even better life. This wonderful future they envisioned revolved around a happy marriage.

(Of course, my parents weren't even happy together, but they refused to get a divorce for years and years. Oh, the irony.)

I certainly don't believe that they key to my happiness is pinning down a perfect husband. I am an independent, career-minded woman. I won't compromise my values or my sense of self just to please a man. At times I feel torn between my desire for a stable, monogamous relationship and my urge to…well, play the field, so to speak. But deep down, I know what I want my future to look like, and it very much resembles the happy marriage and two kids that my parents always promised me I would get.

So for years I was on the dating scene with this in the back of my head, and I'd pull away from every guy who wasn't perfect on paper. No wonder I had such terrible luck—my mom and dad set me up for a load of crap.

Prince Charming my ass!

I've dated my fair share of winners…and losers. I've been engaged twice, and married and divorced once.

Well, *technically,* I'm still married.

Clive, if you're reading this, will you sign those damn papers?

Anyway, my first fiancé, Brian, cheated on me in the worst way possible: with my best friend, Jennifer.

Oh, and he got her pregnant.

Believe it or not, Jennifer was living with us at the time. She was in an abusive relationship and her piece of shit boyfriend beat her up so badly she wasn't recognizable. It was awful. She needed to get out of that situation ASAP, so Brian and I offered to let her stay with us until she got herself together.

Well, as it turned out she was doing more than getting herself together. She was getting with my man—and got herself knocked up!

And how I found out was even crazier. Of course, my women's intuition had already kicked in but I had no solid proof. And never ever would I suspect this bitch who I'd stepped in to help would cross me like that!

Thank goodness for the big mouth receptionist at my local clinic. She told me everything for 100! I walked in for my regular check up and she said, "Your boo came through with his sister the other day."

OK, fine…except Brian had no family in the U.S, so it couldn't have been his sister.

I almost passed out! *Who the fuck did my man accompany to the clinic?* I rushed home and confronted them. They admitted everything and begged for my forgiveness. Can you imagine anything more awkward—or more infuriating—than your fiancé and your best friend telling you about their love child? (If you can, hit me up on Twitter @Tanisha_DaDiva. I'm dying of curiosity.)

Obviously I could have kicked them both out of the house right then and there, but when it comes to infidelity, I try to be a realist. Ladies, I know you don't want to hear it, but we need to face facts: cheating happens. We try to pretend that it doesn't, but men and women cheat all the time—*especially* nowadays, when all it takes is two clicks on an iPhone app to set something up with your sidechick. Try as we might, most of us aren't hard-wired to be monogamous.

In all my experience with disastrous relationships—and believe me, I've had plenty—I've learned that context matters when it comes to cheating. The Who, What, Where, When, Why, and all the Hows: how many times? How drunk was he? How bad does he really feel? Etc, etc, etc. I hate to say it, but there is a gray area where cheating can be acceptable, as long as you are comfortable and able to move on.

Unfortunately, this was not one of those situations. To his credit, Brian apologized repeatedly and swore on his life that it would never happen again, and I really think he meant it. I believed him. So I caved and took him back. I thought I could get past it—but I was wrong.

It wasn't that I didn't trust him. I wasn't snooping through his phone or reading his emails, I felt confident that he was being faithful to me and wouldn't cheat again.

I just didn't *like* the motherfucker anymore.

I mean, I'm not saying you can't cheat! But with my best friend, who we'd taken in under our roof?

Please.

So I woke up one morning and said, "Brian, you gotta go." And that was that.

I started dating Clive shortly after Brian and I broke up. We were kind of seeing each other, nothing official, and then something terrible happened: he woke up one morning and had lost most of his hearing. He spent almost a year in and out of treatment, and for a long time the doctors were just trying to figure out what was wrong. That was a really tough time for him, but it brought us together. I helped take care of him, I slept in the hospital to keep him company, and I stayed by his side. We ended up falling in love, and we stayed together for almost eight years.

My relationship with Clive has been very public, and we've both said and done a lot of things on television that we regret. But we've been through a lot together, and that counts for something. I have a lot of respect for Clive. I was with him when I was living in my mom's basement, when I filmed *Bad Girls Club,* when I went from working at Applebee's to becoming a reality TV superstar. Clive is a good person and for the most part he was kind and supportive, but he never had any ambition and it killed me. Once he realized that he might get famous, it went right to his head. He stopped showing up on time to his job at Pathmark and got demoted from supervisor to a stock boy.

You're trying to tell me you're too good for Pathmark? After all the years you've been finding out about the newest and hottest snacks, you're going to throw shade at Pathmark?

I will take some of the blame, though. When Clive and I were together I wasn't the woman I am now. I was petty, I should have let a lot of stuff go, and I didn't. But you know what? Everything happens for a reason.

Clive and I were engaged for a while, but our relationship was on shaky ground. We took a few breaks, dated other people, and were in the process of reevaluating our decision to spend the rest of our lives together. As if this situation wasn't already complicated enough, out of the blue one day I was pitched the idea for *Tanisha Gets Married.* It would be a one-season BGC spinoff documenting our wedding planning and culminating with the wedding itself.

Great timing, right? I'll be honest: my tanking relationship with Clive notwithstanding, I didn't like the idea at all. I had a really bad feeling about it. You might think that after being on *Bad Girls Club,* which was basically a full season of pure drama, and after getting famous for running around in my pajamas screaming and yelling, I would have no problem taping a show about wedding planning. It seemed pretty benign to most people. But the concept really freaked me out. It's one thing to live in a house with a bunch of strangers, and it's another to invite cameras into your personal life, your home, your family, and your love life. It's a whole different ball game, and it seemed like a huge risk. And to top it all off, Clive and I weren't even sure we wanted to get married right away!

The producers pushed, though, and ultimately Clive and I thought, "What's the worst that can happen?" We decided that we could always film the show but back out of the wedding at the last minute. Having that escape hatch kind of calmed us both down, and we figured a dramatic eleventh hour cancelation would at the very least be good for ratings and make the network happy.

That is, if the eleventh hour cancelation happened.

You see, the plan didn't work out quite the way I had envisioned.

I try to live life with no regrets, I really do. But I wish I could have gotten out of *Tanisha Gets Married.* Obviously Clive and I were not in a good place when that show was presented to us. When I look back on it now, I can't believe we actually went through with it!

This is the number one reason why I try to help the Bad Girls. When I see one of them lose her shit during a reunion, I can relate to that feeling of frustration and guilt. It's a cycle of behaving badly, getting attention for it, and continuing to make bad decisions.

Tanisha Gets Married was one of the hardest shows I've ever done. It was so personal—more than half of the people who were on that show are now completely gone from my life because of the mess it created. There was so much tension, and there were moments during the filming where I was an at all time low. At times I could step outside of myself and think, *This will make a great episode.* If I was one of the producers, I'd probably be thrilled. But it was my *real life.* The cameras were in my mom's house in Flatbush! I couldn't walk away from it at the end of the day: the pandemonium would continue after the cameras stopped rolling, and I had to deal with the fallout.

It just wasn't worth it.

To top it off, despite the nonstop tension and bickering, for some reason Clive backed out on our agreement at the last minute and told me he really did want to get married. I was floored. The producers understood I didn't want to go through with it, but they pointed out that I was going to end up looking like the bad guy if I left Clive at the altar. Call it reality TV stage managing, but they had a point. I mean, would you have liked me if I'd left poor Clive hanging on national television? *I* wouldn't have liked me.

I had two choices. Option Number One: cancel the wedding and deal with the anger and disappointment of the millions of people who watched the show—not to mention Clive. Option Number Two: marry the wrong man and deal with the aftermath privately and on my own terms.

Which did I choose?

Well, neither.

Clive and I did ended up going through with the TV wedding, and we realized immediately that it was a mistake. We got married in December 2011 and by the third week in January he had moved out. Which may sound to you like Option Number Two, except we didn't exactly break up—well, not for a few years, anyway. And we didn't deal with it very privately.

It takes a long time to build up that much history with a person, that much trust and understanding, despite the ups and down. Sometimes it takes a long time to dismantle everything you've worked for in a relationship, say your goodbyes, and move on. The end isn't always a clean break.

Despite the goddamn mess that it caused—well, actually, because of it—*Tanisha Gets Married* was a big success. It debuted with over one million viewers, which made it the networks best performing debut reality series. Compared with Oxygen's time slots that month, it was a 96% increase in the key demographics. It was also one of the most talked about shows on social media at the time. It was clear that people wanted to see our drama play out on television, and that it wouldn't be our last opportunity to do so.

Which leads us to, *Marriage Bootcamp: Reality Stars*. Clive and I weren't living together, but we'd been on-again, off-again for the better part of a year when we were approached by WE to appear on that show. At that point, what did we have to lose? We decided to make one last ditch effort to make it work.

Now, I've been through the emotional ringer on television a handful of times, but *Marriage Bootcamp* took the motherfucking cake. This was a life changing show that prompted me to really examine my behavior and rethink a lot of my decisions. At one point we had to choose someone who had really hurt us in the past and have a conversation with an actor portraying that person.

Who did Clive choose? I'll give you one guess.

Fake Tanisha was pretty much a nightmare. She didn't listen to a word he said, and she just talked *at* him. It was crazy. It was so difficult to watch—I almost couldn't believe that this woman was imitating my behavior. But I had to face the fact that I treated my husband that way.

I honestly thought that Clive and I would be able to work things out. I had started to bounce back, to fall in love with him again. But when I came face to face with what I was doing, I realized there was so much hurt, so much that we'd done to each other. I tried to look past it, but Clive couldn't.

"That girl I first met that I fell in love with, she's not the girl you've been over the past few years," he said. "Part of it is your fault, part of it isn't. You've become so much bigger than the Tanisha that you used to be."

I wasn't sure what to make of that statement—and, honestly, I'm still not sure if I completely understand—but watching Clive go through all of that really prompted me to change, and to let go. I realized that I loved him, but that I needed to love him enough to say goodbye. There was no picking up the pieces of our relationship. We had tried, but we just couldn't make it work.

It was time to move on.

CHAPTER 11

Looking For The One...
Or One Who Will Pay For Dinner

Dear Black Men,

I admire and appreciate your strength, wisdom and courage. You are truly a fearless, relentless warrior. Whatever you put your mind to can and will be conquered...I love you unconditionally and truly value you for all that you do and everything that you are. You are nothing short of amazing.

Now, stop fucking with my head and take me out on a real date.

Love,
Tanisha

★　★　★

I'm just going to go put it out there: when it comes to dating, today's generation has it all wrong. There's no "I want to court you and give you what you deserve."

Men my age want to text all day, "WYD? WYD? WYD?"

Listen up: I'm not doin' you! Obviously because you're texting me dumb shit and honestly I JUST WANT TO GO TO THE MOVIES.

Ladies, I hate to say it, but you're lucky if a man takes you on one date before he tries to get in your pants. You're lucky if you get a slice of pizza. You're lucky if he splits the bill. YOU'RE LUCKY IF HE SHOWS UP.

I'm so sexually frustrated. For some women, a relentless dry spell means they're curling up every night next to a vibrator and a back up supply of batteries. I wish that were the case with me. At least I'd be burning some calories rolling around in bed by myself! No, somehow a total lack of sex means just I'm *starving* all the time. All I want is chocolate! I dream about hot pasta with shrimp. I dream about fresh bread with butter on it. But I don't even want these things! I just need someone to hold me.

So who do I choose, from all of my enticing options?

Let's see. The guy with four baby mommas? The guy who can't get a job?

Listen, I know that it's important to shop around. The pickings might be slim, but we women need to stop settling for what we don't deserve. We need to get up, get out, and keep looking.

This is what I tell myself, at least.

But I keep thinking that the next one will be better—and then the next one turns out to be Satan.

Do you think I'm exaggerating? I'll break it down for you.

When Clive and I broke up, I decided to try online dating. I was overwhelmed at first, but once I got the hang of it, the whole thing was pretty cool. So many fish in the sea, I thought, at least one of them has to be marriage material.

The first guy I met online seemed great. Let's call him Kevin. He had no kids, he was in his twenties, and he had a good job in the trucking business. We started messaging, and he was flirting pretty hard, so after a week or so I started thinking, "When is he going to ask me out?" You see, I don't mind paying for a dating service, but I expect to get my money back in the form of a nice dinner. I let another week go by and then I lost my patience and asked him if he wanted to go on a date.

Kevin's response: "I'm just looking for a really nice girl who doesn't mind coming over. I'll cook for you. We could just eat at the house and chill."

We could just eat at the house and chill.

NEWS FLASH: I DON'T CHILL. That's how you end up with CHILDREN. Better yet, that's how you end up MURDERED.

The Kevin situation brings up two very important points. First off, call me crazy, but there is no way I'm going by myself to the home of a man I've never met before. I'm going to take a second to say that the accusations against Bill Cosby have really thrown me for a loop. I grew up watching *The Cosby Show* and always thought of him as "America's Dad." I get that people are not always who they say they are. But I wanted to believe he was innocent. The fact that it took so long for people to talk about this made me skeptical. But with all these women saying the same thing, famous women who have nothing to gain by going public with their accusations? And the stories are all so similar? How could they all be lying?

Not to be insensitive at all, but men are hunters. That's what they do. They're very aggressive by nature, and it's very hard for them to control themselves around women. Of course, they *should* control themselves, but here's my thing: you don't know what a man is capable of. You don't know what's going on in his head, and you can't assume that he's trustworthy. If a guy is attracted to me and I'm attracted to him, I'm still going to take some time to feel him out and decide if he's safe before I'm alone with him. As strong as I like to think I am, my strength can't match a man's.

Back to Kevin. He invited me over and I thought. *What would I do with this stranger? I don't know him.* I can see the headlines. Can you imagine the headlines if anything had happened to me?

"Dumbass Reality Star Found Dead After Going to Random Internet Boyfriend's House Alone for a First Date."

You've got to be kidding me. The first thing everyone would say is, *What was she thinking?*

He might just want to have an intimate evening chilling out in a comfortable environment. It does make sense on a certain level, but Bill Cosby ruined it for him.

And my next point: the offer to cook for me. Maybe Kevin really is a good cook, but he's not the first man to assume that food is the way to my heart. This is one of the (many) downsides to being a big girl.

Again, I know what he's thinking. *I'll cook her some food, she's a big girl so she'll love it. I'll throw in a few glasses of wine and maybe I'll get lucky.*

Not so fast. Just because I like to eat and am not shy about it doesn't mean that I'll drop my panties for a home cooked meal!

So I told Kevin I would prefer to go out on a real date, not just have sex in his mom's basement, or get murdered, or whatever he had planned for the night.

What did that son of a bitch say?

He said, "I thought we were going to be good together, but I guess not."

He said, "I'm not going to go out and spend money on you. I don't even know if I'm going to like you."

I don't even know if I'm going to like you! Well, that's what first dates are for. First dates that don't take place in your goddamn basement.

Next.

Next up was John. John seemed even more promising than Kevin. He was ex-Army, and he was a calm, cool guy. His body was tight. We went out a few times and I was really digging him… until he revealed that he has two kids, with two different women. I thought, *Okay. I might be able to deal with this.* I mean, I try to keep an open mind. There are a lot of people out there with complicated pasts and difficult family situations, and it's not fair to cast judgment to quickly.

But *then* he told me that some other woman had just appeared out of the woodwork, and that she might be pregnant with his third child.

I've been on a lot of television shows, but I'm not planning on playing out some baby mama drama on *Maury Povich* anytime soon.

Next.

Well, I was thinking *NEXT*. But then John called me and asked me if I knew a loan shark.

"I need $1,200 to buy a car," he said. "Do you know anyone who might lend it to me?"

"Why would I know a loan shark?"

"Well if you don't know a loan shark, do you know anyone who can spare $1,200?"

Okay, okay. He didn't outright ask for the money. But he was hinting. Maybe if he didn't have a litter of children with so many different women, he wouldn't be so hard up for cash.

I try not to be stingy with my money, though, so I seriously considered loaning him the money. John wasn't exactly husband material, but he seemed like a good guy. But then I told one of my friends about the situation and she was shocked.

"Wait, what? You're not offended?" she asked. "You're not even talking to this guy anymore."

I hadn't really thought about it. She was right, though. Whether or not I can afford to give John $1,200 is beside the point. I hardly knew John. He didn't care about me, he didn't add any value to my life. He was just using me.

It amazes me how quick people are to take advantage. It's a slippery slope, too. If you let them walk all over you, they will get comfortable doing it. They will expect more and more, and once you start to push back then you'll look like the bad guy for ending the free ride. Call me stubborn and selfish, but I have to look out for #1. I can't continue to be there for people who aren't there for me.

And, honestly, who does this dude think I am, Oprah?

You get a car! You get a car! Everyone gets a car!

NEXT. NEXT.

Then Shane, a personal trainer, hit me up. "I have a proposition for you. I'll train you for free and we can be FWB."

I'll give you a minute to Google FWB.

Oh fuck it, I'll just tell you what it means: FRIENDS WITH BENEFITS.

This man was just trolling OK Cupid for side chicks. Not to say I've never been a guy's side chick, but it's not something I'm going to go searching for when I'm paying for an online dating service.

At least he was honest…?

Next. Next. Next.

Then for weeks I got caught up texting this guy who seemed so intriguing. We were flirting and getting to know each other and everything seemed great!

Guess what? Once again I ended up in a heap of a mess.

I had convinced myself that we really had something going, and then he stopped responding. I was devastated. I thought to myself, *None of this makes any sense!* I just didn't know what to make of it. He had really seemed…

Hmm…well, once I started thinking about it, there were signs that I shouldn't have taken him seriously.

Signs like him not having a real phone, or never calling me, or not being in a rush to meet me or take me out.

Or that he was clearly insensitive, had the potential to be toxic, and generally seemed like a bad idea.

Somehow I had managed to convince myself that this guy was exactly what I needed.

It's been so long since I've been with a stable, reliable man that I think I might be conditioned to seek out assholes. Or maybe I just get antsy when I find a decent guy. Maybe it's boredom. Because the assholes can be so fucking fun. They're hot, they're good in bed, and the emotional highs and lows can get addicting. It keeps you coming back just when you've made up your mind to walk away—for a while, at least.

I feel like I'm missing something. My friends say, "Stop looking and he'll come to you." But I have to look.

Is he just going to show up at my house?

People say that insanity is doing the same thing over and over and expecting a different result. Does that mean it's insane for me to continue dating? Because I keep meeting the same guy. Sure, they might look different, but it's more or less the same immature man-child over and over.

Either that, or I'm the problem. And if I'm the problem, *then we have a problem*.

I mean, I have my issues and flaws. I get jealous, and I can be stubborn and intimidating. But I can bring a lot to the table! I'm not your average woman. I think outside of the box. When I'm in a relationship, I constantly push my significant other to be better and challenge himself. I love hard, sometimes too hard, but it's because I care.

I'll never let you go to sleep upset. I'll ride for you through all the bullshit as long as you don't bullshit me.

I'm a catch, plain and simple.

I won't buy you a car, though.

CHAPTER 12

Catfished

This son of a bitch is going to get his own chapter.

Do you want to hear about online dating *really* going wrong? I'll tell you about the time I got catfished.

I've watched the MTV series *Catfish,* and honestly, I questioned it. If you haven't seen this show, it's all about how these shady fuckers create fake dating profiles, use other people's photos or lie about themselves, and trick a bunch of lonely, unsuspecting people into falling in love with them.

SMFH.

But to be fair, coming from reality TV, I question everything I watch that claims to be real. It that fake? Is that scripted? How true can these stories really be? For a long time I couldn't imagine that this sort of thing could really be going down in 2015. Catfishing requires the two people to conduct an online-only relationship: no in-person meetings, obviously, and no video chat. How can people go such long periods of time talking online without meeting face-to-face? Not FaceTiming or Skyping? Maybe in 2000, but in this day and age? I just didn't get it.

Until it happened to me.

First off, I want to be clear: technically, I catfish dudes all the time. I'm not using pictures of Beyonce on my profile, I'm tricking these motherfuckers *in person!* I know exactly how to fool a man with some Spanx. My shapewear is like a suit of armor, I'm not kidding. A magical suite of armor. *Now you see it, now you don't! (yes I'm talking about my belly, lol).* You would think I'm another woman altogether. The truth always comes out when we get to the bedroom, but by then, it's too late to turn around and leave!

But this online shit? It's way more deceiving. We all have tricks up our sleeves to make ourselves more attractive in person, but at the end of the day, we have to work with God gave us.

When it comes to the real catfishing, though, the sky is the limit.

Without further ado, here's my real-life catfish horror story.

I met this guy on an online dating site and we started talking. He seemed perfect on paper: a job in the Department of Education, no kids, twenty-nine years old. He was so sweet, so genuine. He called me "Queen." And he was so fine! He looked like a Spanish version of LL Cool J: light skin, muscles, he even wore a Kangol hat.

I know what you're thinking: who is wearing a Kangol hat in 2014? Who is this guy, Samuel L. Jackson? I should have known something was up.

Anyway, it all seemed to good to be true. (Because it was.)

We chatted online for a week or two in late December. We hadn't met yet, but we were just starting to get to know each other a little and everything was going great. Then Christmas Day rolled around and I might have had a little too much wine. It was late in the evening, we'd had a big dinner and my family had gone to bed. I was sitting by myself in my mom's living room when this dude messaged me. We texted a bit and then he said he wanted to come see me. He knew that we lived in the same neighborhood in Brooklyn.

"It's a ten minute walk," he said. "I don't mind."

I know, I know: this whole situation violates my usual rules. Letting a total stranger, a guy who might be a serial killer, into my house? Not demanding a nice date first? Yeah, not the smartest. But to be fair, my family was upstairs. If anything bad happened I could just scream and my crazy ass mom would be on the scene! And I did want to meet him in person. It was Christmas night and I was feeling lonely. I was thinking, we'll just have a drink, talk for a bit, and maybe make out. I started smiling to myself just thinking about him.

I thought, no harm done.

Also, I was a little drunk.

So I agreed, and he came to my house about forty minutes later.

Oh my God.

Alcohol is the craziest thing. It can make you make the dumbest decisions. It allows you to justify shit that you would never even consider doing normally. But when things don't go to plan, you sober up, *immediately*.

My drunk ass was on cloud nine that night, waiting for this guy to come over. And then he showed up and WHAT A BUZZKILL! Here I was expecting LL Cool J and out comes Chuy from *Chelsea Lately! I almost passed out!* Not to be mean. But it's the truth.

Now, I think the photos I'd seen were actually of him. But they were either photoshopped, or he has some kind of funhouse mirror in his apartment. Because there was nothing in his profile pictures that indicated he was less than five feet, eight inches! He looked completely different than in the pics!

I think I've eaten bigger sandwiches than this guy.

So Bite Sized was at my door, and I didn't know what to do.

I realized I just needed to stay calm and not draw attention to it. I was literally talking to myself. *Be nice. Don't be rude. Don't show how you feel inside. You don't have to marry this guy, you just have to talk to him.*

And to his credit, he was a total gentleman. We talked for an hour or so, and then I yawned loudly, told him I needed to go to bed, and saw him out the door.

End of story? I wish. Sure, nothing romantic happened that night but he still had every reason to believe I was interested. He kept trying to contact me, and I just didn't know what to do.

"I think we're best off as friends," I said, hoping to break it to him as gently as possible. "You're a great guy and I would love to be friends with you."

His reply: "Oh. That's not exactly what I had in mind."

Well, you want to know what I had in mind? A man who is taller than my three-year-old niece.

He does seem like a great guy, though. I wasn't lying! He told me everything I wanted to hear, everything I've been hoping a man would say to me these past few years. He was sensitive and funny. He wanted commitment, he wanted to take me on vacation, he listened to me and respected me.

Of course, right? This totally makes sense. The man who would love me and treat me well happens to be five foot nothing and I'm not remotely attracted to him.

I'm always in love with what I cannot have. I don't know what that says about me, but it's the truth. The guys that would walk to the end of the earth for me? I'm like, get away.

But the guy who will treat me like crap, break my heart and make me cry? The men who make no effort, who never call, who creep around on their girlfriends? Somehow I find them irresistible.

How is this happening? I thought. I realized I could try to force myself to date this guy, but in my gut I knew it wasn't going to work.

I had to move on. But before I make any rash decisions I turn to Instagram.

Sometimes you just need a second opinion. And while there are definitely some haters on my feed, I have a lot of love for my Instagram followers. I don't even consider them fans. I consider them friends—and they give the best advice.

So I put the question out there for the ladies: Would you date a guy who is shorter than you?

There were some dissenting opinions, but the general consensus was NO. Does that mean we're shallow? Maybe. But a lot of my followers made a great point: if you're a dominant, aggressive woman, it's important for you to feel like your man is strong and powerful. When it comes to personality, you probably tower over him, so you don't want to feel like you're physically bigger, too.

I know I've talked a lot about men being overly critical of women's bodies and holding us to an unattainable standard. I'm not saying that my man needs to look like a male model. But physical attraction is so important. It's essential to a healthy relationship. You can't pull it out of thin air—it has to come naturally. And when there's no chemistry, you have to recognize that and learn to walk away. Otherwise, it's not fair to either of you.

Plus, that little dude catfished me, so fuck him.

CHAPTER 13

Tips From The
Dating Trenches

When it comes to dating, I've seen it all. I've made some decisions I regret, and I've seen some shit that I wish I could unsee. Let's just say I've learned a thing or two . . . or ten.

Here are a few tips to help you avoid making the same mistakes as me:

- Don't automatically give a man your all—make him work for it.
- Learn to recognize when a man just isn't good enough for you. Trust your gut. Sometimes you just need to face facts! The bad guys are often intriguing—and they're almost always good in bed—but they're still BAD.
- Once you realize that he's not right for you, kick him to the motherfucking curb. Block his phone number, unfollow him on Instagram, unfriend him on Facebook, and don't

look back. The wrong man will not only block the RIGHT one, but all of your blessings as well.

- When a man has decided who he wants (and it's not you) you're not going to convince him otherwise, no matter how many twerk moves and home cooked meals are in your arsenal, Happy relationships are never a constant struggle. What is for you, will not pass you—so don't fight so hard for something that isn't working.
- Have a seat in the passenger side. It's ok to not be in control all of the time. Allow a man to be a Man.
- Sometimes you're better off being friends. Just because you're the opposite sex doesn't mean you have to *have sex*.
- If things don't work out, don't always assume it's his fault.

Here are three signs that you're not ready to be in a relationship:

- Lack of self-confidence: A lot of women talk the talk about being confident—and then they let men walk all over them. No one will love you if you don't love yourself. Don't let your standards slip: don't let a man stand you up or take you to McDonald's and call it a date. What you allow is what will continue. Sometimes you have to demand respect, and the more you let a man disrespect you, the more comfortable he's going to get treating you that way. You have to learn how to set those standards because no one is going to set them for you.

- You're on the rebound: Make sure you're over your last relationship before you start a new one. I know it's hard because he was so great in bed, but at the end of the day you need to get it out of your system before you start fresh. It's not fair to you, and it's not fair to the next person. Don't go after the same guy that's causing you heartbreak; that's the definition of insanity. If you're not comfortable being alone and being single, you won't be happy in a relationship.

- You have trust issues: This is a tough one. Trust issues are understandable. I can relate: it's hard for me to believe that nothing is happening if there's a pretty girl hovering around my man. But you can't live your life being paranoid. It will make you insane to read his texts and emails 24/7, and it will be detrimental to your relationship. (He probably has a separate creep line, anyway. JK!)

- Stop having one night stands! You make it bad for women who hold out a little bit. Listen, I don't have sexual hang ups. I know who I am, I'm a grown woman, and when it comes to sex I am comfortable doing whatever I want to do. I'm not putting a time frame on it, but not the first night! You're devaluing yourself and you're devaluing your relationship with this man.

- Live with a man before you marry him. Be sure you know the ins and outs of his personality before you decide to be together forever. You will have to listen

to him snore and watch him scratch his balls FOR THE
REST OF YOUR LIFE.

◆ Your man will probably have some annoying habits.
Maybe he talks while he chews, maybe he wears the
wrong shoes. As long as he respects and loves you,
they don't need to be deal breakers.

◆ If you're having no luck with the bar scene or online
dating, try new activities. Take a cooking class, go to
a different gym. Have a friend set you up. Hell, keep
your eyes peeled in the grocery store!

◆ Who the fuck cares what anyone else thinks? I
remember when I broke up with Clive only six weeks
after our wedding, my friends said, "You better keep
this secret, you can't let anybody know." You know
what? Our breakup was absolutely nobody's business,
but I will not keep up a front just to save face. If it's
not working out, it's not working out. It happens to the
best of us and there's nothing to be ashamed of. Off to
the next we go just like J.Lo.

CHAPTER 14

Money And Envy

I probably haven't met you, but you should know this: I want to see you do good. I hope that you succeed in all of your endeavors, that you have a family and a partner who love you, and that you feel good about yourself.

I want to see everybody do good!

Now, is that so hard? Why can't we all feel this way?

Listen up: Envy is one terrible, green-eyed bitch. We don't need that hoe! I'm amazed at how competitive and jealous people can be. I am in constant disbelief at how quick women in particular are to bring each other down—especially in Hollywood. There are women out there who see each other as rivals when they should be allies, and who think that the only way to the top is by pushing someone else to the bottom.

Over the past few years, I've had to lean hard on two invaluable lessons I learned from my dad:

1) Material things don't make you a better or happier person.
2) Jealousy should motivate you, not make you bitter and angry.

Words to live by! They seem like common sense, but believe me, they can be hard pills to swallow.

I learned about gratitude and contentment at a young age. When I was in elementary school, I had a friend who seemed to have everything under the sun. Every toy, every doll. She had the Barbie with the convertible *and* Barbie's little sister! I was so jealous.

This girl had a birthday party at her house one day, and a dozen of us spent the afternoon in her living room playing with her toys.

Well, to be totally accurate, *I* spent the entire party taking a mental inventory of all of the things that she had, and I worked myself up into a frenzy of jealousy. I was so upset that I couldn't concentrate on hanging out with my friends.

I had a miserable time.

My dad picked me up at her house and I pouted the whole ride home. Daddy humored me for a few minutes, but it was clear that he wanted to get to the bottom of my behavior.

"Do you want to talk about it?" he asked after driving for a while in total silence.

"No," I said. "I just want an M&M."

This was a game we used to play all the time: he would keep one M&M in his shirt pocket and ask me to guess what color it was. The winner would get to eat it.

He *always* won.

Hmm…come to think of it, that seems a little suspicious.

Anyway, my dad wasn't in the mood to play the M&M game that day. "Tanisha, you don't want candy," he said. "You're clearly upset about something and you need to deal with it. Are you pouting because Samantha had some new toys?"

"She didn't have *some* toys," I insisted. "She had *all the toys in the world.*"

(Drama queen from an early age, I know.)

Then my dad explained to me that Samantha was actually very sick. I was too young and self-absorbed to read the signs.

"You know how you can go outside and run around and do what you want?" he said. "She can't do that because she's sick. Her parents buy her these toys to make it up to her."

"I didn't know that," I said.

"That's OK, honey," he told me. "But now you know. You should be happy for people who have things that you want. You never know what storm God put them through."

And that's how I learned to always focus on what I have, not on what I don't have.

That everything that glitters—even the stupid Barbie convertible—is not gold.

★ ★ ★

The truth is, I would have been so mean and harsh without my dad. He helped me smooth over so many of my rough edges when it comes to dealing with people. He taught me everything I know about handling my money and focusing on what's really important in life.

My dad was the sweetest, most emotionally generous person in the entire world. But he was also as frugal as it gets. He was

West Indian, and being an immigrant in the United States shaped his attitude toward money and ambition. He and my mom worked hard to provide a good life for me in their adopted country.

I'm from a working-class part of Brooklyn, but my story isn't exactly rags to riches. Before I was on television I always had a job. I waitressed, I worked as a nurse's aid for the City of New York. I had benefits, I made decent money, and I never struggled. But my dad always encouraged me to save.

"Save your money," he said. "You have to be cautious, you never know what's going to happen. Save it for a rainy day."

My father told me to only ever spend forty percent of what I make. That's been a rule of thumb for me my whole life. And it hasn't changed, even as I've become more famous over the years.

In Hollywood, the pressure to throw your money around is unreal. When you live your life in the public eye, it's easy to get caught up in a flashy lifestyle. Everyone around you is spending money on clothes and bags, blowing thousands of dollars in the clubs. And you want to look your best. There are pictures of you pumping gas in magazines and on the internet!

But you know what's scary to me? Seeing people who used to be big stars, people that I admired and wanted to emulate, who don't look so good these days. Now, I don't think these celebrities have just decided to start saving for a rainy day. It makes me wonder: what could you have possibly done with your money? Now, I don't want to talk shit, but someone like Faith Evans? I have a lot of respect for her, but honestly, she doesn't look like she ever made money in her life. It's scary. Even if you're bringing in beaucoup dollars today, you can't assume that the money will still be rolling in tomorrow.

I'm lucky that my family has kept me in check, and that I've had financial responsibilities that have kept me from burning through every dollar I've earned. I promised my brother early on that I would pay for his college tuition, and I was able to come through for him. When my dad was sick, I took care of him. It was important for me to support my family.

I never try and keep up. Listen, there's nothing wrong with spoiling yourself, but I don't need to buy more stuff. The happiness you get from a shopping spree just doesn't last.

I get so tired of *things*.

Can I wear high end shit and stunt all day and night? Sure. Could I be pushing a Benz and living in a high rise in the city? Absolutely. Could I spend $600 on shoes? Honey, my shoes are already doing me a favor! I don't need to put that pressure and ruin an expensive good shoe.

But it's more important to me to create a life that feels good on the inside, not one that looks good on the outside. I don't let material possessions validate who I am. Never did, never will. The way I see it, I'm already one of the cool kids! I make things cool, not the other way around.

I have long term goals that are more important than looking like a million bucks right now, and I do everything at my OWN pace. So screw you if my glasses look too nerdy for you or my car isn't German. I would rather spend my money on experiences: on a nice vacation, the best seats for a show, a delicious dinner. Things that can be remembered.

They mean so much more.

And at the end of the day I love my coins right where I can see them: *in the motherfucking bank.*

Not everyone in my life feels this way. I can tell my mother that I love her till I am blue in the face but she doesn't believe me until I buy her a present. That's her love language. When I buy her gifts she'll tear up, she'll be excited and cherish it, but she won't hug me.

I can't really blame her, though. It must have something to do with her childhood. She grew up fairly poor, and possessions made her very happy. They give her a sense of security and comfort. I don't know what that's like because when I was growing up we never lacked for things.

And the truth is, my mom would give me the shirt off her back. She's just not as vocal about it.

I started talking to her about my late father on Christmas Day this year. I always miss him a lot over the holidays, and he'd been on my mind all day. I was very close with my father, but his relationship with my mom was always kind of a mystery to me. My parents never seemed very happy together, but even though things didn't work out between them, I know my mom loved him very much. She'd just never opened up to me about it.

So this Christmas I asked her to tell me the story of how she met my dad. Not only did I want to share in his memory for a little, I also wanted to know how she managed to snag a man like him. (I mean, I need all the help I can get, and my dad was one hell of a catch.)

She was reluctant to share. "Tanisha, you're being nosy," she said.

"Mom, I'm feeling a little lost in my life right now," I explained. "I just wish I had some stories to draw reference to, to help guide me. Maybe you could give me some insight."

She paused for a long time.

"Daddy would want you to," I said.

So she finally opened up to me. It was the best Christmas present I could have asked for.

I constantly hear my dad's voice. Every time I feel that pang of jealousy I hear him. I just have to push harder, I have to move on.

It's not my blessing.

We need to congratulate people for doing well. We need to use jealousy to motivate us to work harder, not to sit back and judge people or resent them. Everything is possible if you're willing to do the work. You have to take the negative and turn it into a positive.

When it comes to coping with jealousy, it can be hard for me to put my money where my mouth is.

I'll let you in on a little secret. Do you know that show *The Real?* The talk show that is a younger, more entertaining, and more diverse version of *The View?* The show that's on television *every damn day?*

I was almost cast on that show. I pretty much had it in the bag!

I've worked with the executive producer, Sally Ann Salsano, many times and she called me first about being on *The Real*. What an opportunity! I was super excited but didn't know who else they were considering or how big it would potentially be. But then my manager called to remind me that I was locked into a contract with Oxygen, so I'd have to turn it down. She expected me to be freak out. But I wasn't mad.

How could I be mad about my contract with Oxygen? The network that gave me my start in this business?

You see, it's just not my blessing. For whatever reason, this is how it's supposed to be.

"Let's work," I said to my manager. "Let's get something else."

Next thing I knew, I had an offer for a new project. So there you go.

CHAPTER 15

The Best Show I Ever Hosted, On The Worst Day Of My Life

I've lived through a failed marriage (on television, no less) and about a thousand bad boyfriends, but I didn't know real heartbreak until my father passed away.

My father was hardworking, kind, and always supportive. He was just an incredible man, plain and simple. Even when I was at my worst he was always proud of me. He's the reason I'm so confident, and he's the model for my future husband. I might be too picky thanks to my dad, but that's fine by me.

Daddy left us in 2012. It wasn't sudden; he was sick for a while, and then he had a stroke. But I was devastated.

To make matters worse, my father's illness and death coincided with a whole bunch of family drama that I had been trying to distance myself from. My dad has another set of kids from his first marriage. All my siblings have traditional careers, are well-to-do and successful, and our family is very competitive. Over the years we've had our fair share of conflict, and I've had to stop speaking to a lot of family. It was part of my healing process, but I had to let them go.

My relationship with my oldest half-sister is particularly strained. She always resented my dad for marrying my mom, and she was very jealous of our relationship. In my father's eyes, I could do no wrong, and that wore on her over the years.

I wish I could say that my sister and I came together when Daddy's health started failing, but unfortunately, the tension mounted. As the oldest, she was named my dad's proxy. We often disagreed on how to handle things, but she called the shots, and I had no say in the matter. I was traveling to L.A. to film on a regular basis at the time, when I returned to Brooklyn after one trip I found out that my sister had had him placed in a nursing home.

It killed me to see him in the home, and it killed me to leave him and go back to L.A. It was a terrible time for him, and for me. It was really, really hard to do what I wanted to do and still be there for my family. My sister did everything in her power to shut me out of his caretaking decisions.

I've never felt so powerless.

I was so mad at myself. I kept thinking, *I should be able to fight this.*

The second half of this one-two punch was a major falling out with my cousin, who had been like a sister to me (well, a sister that I actually got along with!) Growing up, we were best friends and confidantes. We were as tight as can be—until I started to become famous. That's when everything changed.

During the height of my career, she and I took a girls' vacation to St. Martin. I had been looking forward to the trip for months. Sun, sand, endless piña-coladas, and picking up cute guys, right? Well, that's how it went for a day or two, until she up and lost it on me. She told me that I was different, that we had grown apart, that I had turned Hollywood and didn't care about her anymore

"I'm the same person now," I insisted. "I'm just a little more popular."

But she wouldn't listen to me, and there was nothing I could do to convince her otherwise.

Her words cut deep, and for a while after that trip I seriously questioned myself. I worried that I was changing, that I was distancing myself from my loved ones. I talked to a lot of people that I respected and trusted during that time.

I called up my former manager, who was a close friend of mine. I started crying—I was bawling my eyes out. But he reassured me that what I felt in my heart was true: I was still the same old Tanisha. Brash, honest, loving, and down to earth.

"Tanisha, you're working," he told me. "You're not changing."

He gave me this incredible advice, which I will never forget: "Never, ever let someone tell you you're doing something wrong when you're working toward bettering yourself."

I realized that the higher I climbed in regards to my career, the more people I would lose. It's unfortunate, it's messed up, but it's the truth.

People want to see you doing good, until you're doing *too* good.

And if people are going to turn their backs on you because they are jealous, you have to recognize that those aren't the type of people that you want in your life.

I knew that my dad would agree.

In the end, I had to accept that my cousin's accusations were a reflection of her own issues, and the only thing I could do was give her time and space and hope that she would come around. Sometimes, when you just can't get through to a person, you just have to be patient.

Daddy passed away the day before we filmed the reunion episode for season ten of BCG. I got out of a meeting and saw that I had about a dozen missed calls, and I just knew.

I took it hard—honestly, to this day I don't even think I've fully dealt with the fact that he's gone. I felt like I was alone and I didn't have anybody. The one person in this world I could turn to was gone, and I didn't get to say goodbye.

I kept thinking, *I would give everything up just to see him again.* I just didn't know how I would pick up the pieces. And I certainly didn't know how I was going to be able to host the reunion in twenty-four hours. My father would have wanted me to pull it together, though. He was always my number one fan, and I knew I had to show up the next day so that I wouldn't disappoint him.

At this point, it would be nice to think that my dysfunctional family finally pulled together.

It would be nice, but it's not true.

My father was a strict Seventh-day Adventist. In accordance with his religious beliefs, he wanted to be buried, but my brother and sister insisted on cremating him to save money. I put my foot down; I had to. Daddy deserved to be honored and memorialized the way he wanted. It was the least we could do.

So there I was, the morning of the reunion taping, sitting in the make up chair and arguing with my siblings on the goddamn phone about my father's burial.

"I will be out of touch for six hours," I finally told them. "Do not touch Daddy for six hours. Don't worry about the money. When I'm done, I will deal with this."

When I stepped out onto the set, I was shaking with anger and grief. I sat in my chair, took a deep breath, and waited for the cameras to start rolling.

Tanisha's on in 5 . . . 4 . . . 3 . . . 2 . . . 1

Season Ten: Atlanta was one of the craziest seasons of BGC ever, and some of the girls showed up at the reunion with a big fucking axe to grind. I hadn't even finished greeting all the girls at the beginning of taping when Shannon bum rushed the stage and started a full on catfight. Rocky joined in to help her and things got really heated. The security guards swarmed the place. Valentina toppled over and cut open her forehead.

It was a hot rotisserie mess!

The audience looked a little freaked out, and I desperately needed to lighten things up. So I offered the girls a slice of pie from my snack bag, and when they ignored me I started eating whipped cream straight from the container. The audience cracked up.

When the dust settled, though, I ended up with Valentina being rushed to the hospital, Rocky and Shannon in a time out in a dressing room, three of the six girls on stage, and a live studio audience twiddling their thumbs.

"They don't pay me enough for this," I said.

But I got the room back under control. I jumped back into the reunion, brought the energy up, and returned to the regularly scheduled program.

I had to rise above so much that day. I had to put aside my grief, my anger and frustration, and focus on my job. And the funny thing is, I was on fire: I've never been funnier, quicker, or more full of energy. I had a light in me. It was one of the best reunions I've ever hosted—on one of the worst days of my whole life. I swear, my father was with me throughout the taping, encouraging me and guiding me. And for that I am forever grateful.

CHAPTER 16

BFFs Forever

What do a straight-laced businesswoman, an ordained pastor, a hair stylist, and a professional photographer all have in common?

They're my best friends.

We can't choose our family, but THANK THE LORD we can choose our friends—because mine are everything to me. We don't always see eye-to-eye most of the time, but they give me the best advice, they provide a great example for me, they listen to me and inspire me. It makes all the difference in the world to have the love and support of my friends.

You might remember Bella from *Tanisha Gets Married.* She was one of my bridesmaids on the show, and luckily she's not one of the people who stopped talking to me after we finished taping. She's my best friend. Bella is just awesome: she's an amazing makeup artist, she's smart, she's business-driven, and she's very successful at what she does. She's a beautiful girl with a regal presence who used to only date millionaires, but has now settled down with a nice guy.

In some respects, we couldn't be more different. Bella is straight-laced and reserved, and I'm—well, you know how I am by now. I'll put it this way: if we were designer clothes, Bella would be Tom Ford and I would be Betsy Johnson.

But even though we speak at different volumes, our message is often the same. We're both honest, we call out people's bullshit, we think alike business wise, we speak our mind, she really brings out the best in me and she helps me find clarity.

I can be very hard on myself but she tells me it's fine: you live and you learn. I love her for that.

What have I learned from Bella?

Live it up, it's your life. Do what you want to do and BE HAPPY.

Then there's Janel. Janel is an ordained pastor and a hugely successful hairstylist. She thinks I'm batshit crazy, but she loves me. Janel forces me to hold myself accountable for my actions and is a big inspiration for me. She's so honest, and so insightful.

For as strong as her religious beliefs are, Janel doesn't push them on me. She understands that I have my own personal spirituality and relationship with God.

She does, however, tell it like it is.

Janel appeared on an episode of *David Tutera CELEBrations* with me. David was throwing me a divorce party, and at the last minute everything started to go wrong. I hated all the dress options, time was ticking, and I was just all around annoyed. I was so frustrated I was ready to cancel the party.

While David's team was trying to sort everything out, my close friend Amber, made a pretty weird suggestion on behalf of Janel.

"Hey Tanisha," she said. "Janel thought maybe you should take a shower so you can feel fresh."

"I'm not going to shower *now,*" I told her, totally annoyed. "I took a shower this morning."

Amber seemed kind of flustered—she's this cute little blue eyed girl with no poker face whatsoever—and she kept insisting. "Don't you want to take, like...a little shower?" At that point I was eyeing Amber like that girl with the hand turned palm face up in all the Instagram memes.

The next thing I know Janel peeks through the door and is like, um, just take the damn shower.

I'm like why? Do I really need to?

She's like yes you are hot, sweaty and yes.

Now if that's not a real friend, I don't know what is! A lot of people would have taken that the wrong way. But I was so grateful for my friends' brutal honestly all I could do was lather up and laugh.

So I took a shower and I wasn't sweaty anymore, and I ended up having a great time. Because you know what? That's what friends are for. To tell you to take a shower because you're sweating like a pig.

Then there's Genevieve or as everyone likes to call her "G." G owns a celebrity hair salon in Brooklyn. She's had it tough: she's never had a lot of luck with people, a lot of her friends have done her wrong, and at some point she had to clean up shop and get rid of everyone who had been toxic in her life. G and I have been through a lot of similar struggles in our personal lives: we've both dealt with a lot of bad romantic relationships, and she also has a strained relationship with her mom.

Although she got her mom to go to therapy and it has worked wonders for their relationship. I wish I could get my whole family in therapy, but Caribbean people don't believe in it! If I asked my mom to go with me, she'd curse me out. She thinks that going to a therapist means that you're insane.

Shit, I think you're crazy if you *don't* go to therapy.

Anyway, G and I clicked from day one. I came into her salon to get my hair done and she just started pouring her heart out to me. People always tell me that I make them feel comfortable, that they feel like they've known me for years even if we've just met. G *definitely* had that feeling: she opened up to me about the terrible breakup she was going through, she was hopelessly in love with this girl and was so confused about how to move forward. She was crying her eyes out while she was supposed to be doing my hair! But that's LOVE for you. It never really gives a fuck.

Now, we both know that I've been there, and I can't always say that I've stayed strong in these types of situations. I'm still in touch with an ex who I want so badly, but I have to tell myself every day that he doesn't love me.

When someone hurts you and they don't apologize, that's someone who doesn't care about you. End of story. Even if I have trouble taking my own advice, I had to keep it real with Genevieve.

I told her to walk away and not look back. "There's nothing to think about," I said.

A little tough love goes a long way. I told her to face facts and to stop making excuses, and the next think I knew she was like my sister.

When Genevieve finally found the right girl, she almost missed it. She was still torn up about her ex. She was so scared, so afraid and so insecure that she couldn't even recognize when a good thing came her way.

"You need to snap out of it," I told her. "You have to give this girl a chance."

And Genevieve was a hot mess when they started dating, but you know what? They love each other and they're happy.

How many times have you found yourself at home on a Friday night crying over your ex when all your friends are turning up?

Listen, I'm going to cry. If I loved you and it's over, it's going to hurt and I'm going cry. But that's what waterproof mascara is for!

Because, guess what? Your ex is somewhere else having a great time.

Am I going to let him laugh while I'm crying? Nope—I'm going to keep it moving.

Last but not least, there's Nez. Nez is a fan turned friend. He offered to do photography for me through social media, I took him up on his offer, and we've been inseparable ever since.

I've learned a lot from Nez, but most of all, he's provided a model for the happy marriage I hope to have one day.

Nez and I go everywhere together. If I were his wife, I would *not* be happy about my husband spending so much time with another woman. Nez and I do events together, and we're out until all hours of the night. It'll be 4 a.m. and I'll look at him and say,

"How is your wife not beefing? How can she trust you like this?"

"Where would I go?" he asks. "I know what I have at home."

At the end of the night he's going home to his wife and his five kids.

I see why. Nez's wife trusts him. She never looks through his phone. She's so patient and kind. She exudes everything that a real woman is supposed to be.

I'm not there yet. If the roles were reversed I'd be accusing him of cheating. But I look up to her.

I hope to be half the woman she is one day. One day—but NOT today.

My BGC sisters Amber Meade and Shay Calhoun are also two friends that I couldn't survive without. Amber and I are really kids at heart. Seriously, hide your knives and anything fragile because with us two around anything can happen. I love my little vanilla sundae I love to think of us as the ultimate dessert: she's the fluffy soft serve with whipped cream and a cherry, and I'm the caramel and nuts on top. Together we are the perfect blend of wtf?! with a smile.

Then there's Shay. Shay and I met while I was at a taping for *Dancing with the Stars*. I was on my way to use the bathroom and she stopped me dead in my tracks.

"Um, don't I know you?" she asked.

I started to screw up my face a bit trying to remember from where when she blurted out, "Don't give me that face." I laughed and was instantly in love with her larger than life persona. Shay is probably the most influential person in my life and doesn't even realize it. She gives me priceless wisdom, encouragement and tough love even when I don't want to hear it.

I couldn't ask for better BFFs. Hopefully they all feel the same about me.

CHAPTER 17

Thirty Days—and a Lifetime— to a Better Me

I'm a great listener and can talk just about anyone off the ledge in a crisis—just ask any of my friends—but I'm terrible at taking my own advice.

I heard about auditions for *Girlfriend Intervention* while I was taping *Marriage Bootcamp*. They were looking for a soul coach for a modern day makeover squad. It seemed right up my alley, a chance to work with my love for fashion and help well-deserving women get their confidence back by making them over from the inside out.

I was up against some heavy hitters for the spot on *Girlfriend Intervention*. I won't name names, but I'm talking about some women that I have admired for years! When I left the audition, I called my manager and told her I didn't think I got it.

"But Tanisha, you're always sure!" she said.

"Not this time," I told her. "I'm really not sure."

So when I got the call, I was shocked. I was blessed to be a part of this show. It's just feel-good TV, and it's amazing to see women get their confidence back and transform before our very eyes, over coming body image issues, low self-esteem, and fear of failure. I love helping the moms in particular: a lot of these ladies have so much on their plates, juggling family and careers, that they often stop taking care of themselves and they lose their sense of self-worth. It's truly rewarding to help inspire their inner glow.

Unfortunately, *Girlfriend Intervention* faced a whole lot of backlash before it even aired! The first season of the show is about black women helping white women, and a lot of people criticized us for reinforcing racial stereotypes.

I thought that every woman would embrace and support this uplifting show but, honey, surprisingly, some of my sisters were very upset with me. I kept getting messages about, girl, now you know us sisters need help too I'm saying! They don't want us helping white women get a man? Girl, if he left you for her, then he was never yours in the first place!

But here's the most important thing. Our message applies to *all* women. And yeah, we made over white women in the first season, but I would love to open up the show to women of all different backgrounds. The message is really universal. It's about female empowerment for women of all colors and all shapes and sizes.

When I think about my career long-term, I think about the powerful and positive message that reality TV can have. I love being on TV, but eventually I would like to focus my time and energy on creating and producing genuine, realistic, and entertaining content that helps people better themselves. I'm telling you I'm not the cold ruthless bitch everyone proclaims me to be! I'm actually very sensitive and empathetic to others. A mama bear if you will.

So you see, Mama Bear Tanisha loves to give advice...But as for taking it? Well, let's just say, It's been a long road.

I'm going to share one last terrible dating story. Meet Tony. Tony was an assistant director on a show that I was hired to host. We met on set and, although the sparks didn't fly immediately, there was just something about him. Now there were distinct rules that prohibited the crew from ever dating talent but I just knew something about our connection couldn't be stopped. We wrapped the show and almost immediately went out on a date. It was magical! I mean besides the fact that he took me to one of my favorite places on earth (*Cirque de Soleil*), I was just so into him that night.

Something about watching folks twirl in the air with sparkly costumes had me feeling "some type of way." Or maybe it was the cognac my date decided to get for me. It wasn't long before I spilled my drink a bit down my dress and Tony decided he would get that mess up for me. It was that moment I knew. He was going to be mine!

I don't need to get into all the details, but we started an on-again, off-again relationship that lasted for two years and ended up being incredibly toxic. Tony was very abusive to me in many ways. I just didn't see it in the beginning, and it took me a long time to stand up for myself and break the cycle. I finally ended it.

I know what you're thinking: with this no-good man out of my life, things started looking up, right?

Honey, don't you know about the curse? When it comes to love, nothing is that simple for me.

My breakup with Tony really messed me up. I started going through a deep, dark depression. I hate to say it, but I missed him. I also started questioning a lot of things about my life in general. Remember that old vision of the happy marriage, handful of kids, and unstoppable career? I thought Tony might be a part of that perfect life. I thought I was working toward what my life should be. But with him gone the whole thing just toppled like a house of cards.

A few things helped me come to my senses.

First, I went to dinner with my friend Shae and her fiancé, Dante, in L.A. They pretty much had to drag me out of my hotel room that night: I was feeling so sorry for myself and I didn't want to go anywhere. I just wasn't myself.

At dinner I confessed that I was having Tony withdrawals. I was feeling so desperate—I was ready to call an Über and show up at his apartment and beg him to take me back!

Dante responded with some serious tough love. He said, "Tanisha, you'll never be 'good enough' for a man who isn't ready. This has nothing to do with you. It's no longer your battle. He's not ready and he needs to fix himself. Let go, let God take it from here."

This isn't my battle.

He made me say it out loud!

After dinner I went back to my hotel and deleted Tony's number from my phone. That was step one.

Then shortly after that night I did a radio interview. I was still feeling pretty low at the time.

"Tanisha, you're really making something for yourself," the host said. "You're taking a reality TV career and turning it into an empire. You are everywhere! And it's smacking to watch so, who is Tanisha Thomas?"

I'm rarely speechless, but I didn't know what to say. I could not answer that question.

In that moment I realized that I had lost sight of my identity as a strong, funny, smart, and successful person. I didn't know who I was anymore.

The phone lines were blazing up with people calling, asking me questions about being confident and curvy.

I couldn't believe it. The sad thing is, it took a woman I didn't even know to give me a wake up call.

It's amazing how strangers will support you, more so than the people in your life—and more than you will support yourself.

What I came to understand is that people only treat you in ways that you allow. By letting Tony treat me like shit and taking him back so many times, I was simply telling him, "This is how I want to be treated. Keep it coming."

The longer I let that happen, the more I lost sight of what true love actually is.

Sometimes I think I'm addicted to love. I crave love, I want it, I need it. Love is a beautiful thing. But true love is not a reason to sacrifice your own happiness, to tolerate disrespect, or to forgive someone who fails you. True love accepts you the way you are. It makes you a better person without asking you to change. It's unconditional. That's what makes it such a beautiful thing.

After that day I decided to revamp my life. I started working on me and started the #IAMCHALLENGE on social media to share my journey with my followers. Every day for the next thirty days I would reevaluate my life and I devoted each day to a different challenge: Determination, Accountability, Resilience, etc.

Forgiveness was a big one for me. Forgiving myself, accepting the mistakes that I've made and giving myself a pat on the back for trying.

It was hard, and it was intense, but it really helped.

And it didn't end after a month. It's changed my outlook for taking things day by day.

Give it a try. It starts in the morning. In the morning you decide what type of day you'll have. I get up every single morning and I read inspirational quotes. I look in the mirror and I tell myself, "You are enough, there is nobody like you. You are unique, you are creative, go kill it today."

I say that to myself EVERY SINGLE MORNING! And it really sets the tone for the rest of my day.

You have to remember that this is your life. You're in control, you're the CEO. You get to decide what happens next.

People are going to deny you. People are going to tell you no almost every single day. Even if it seems like there's no hope, you have to find a way. If a door doesn't open, then bust open some windows.

Don't expect others to understand your dreams when God didn't give them your vision.

Guess who called me up out of the blue while I was in the middle of doing all this work on myself?

Of course, Tony.

He wanted to meet up. In the spirit of forgiveness, I decided to meet him for coffee. We chatted for a while and he said, "I love this new Tanisha. Where was she the whole time we were dating?"

He wanted to give it another try. And honey, I would by lying to you if I said I wasn't tempted. He seemed genuine, he seemed willing to appreciate me and try to work on our communication. I started thinking that Tony and Tanisha version 2.0 might work.

But something wasn't sitting right.

I was a different and improved version of myself. Tony came back the same old Tony.

I had lost a lot of me in that relationship. I was really damaging myself and suppressing who I was to make him happy.

I'm so much better off without him.

But you know what the funny thing is about rock bottom?

It hurts like hell, but it's a beautiful place to start fresh.

CHAPTER 18

Rules To Live By

In the last year I've learned that there are no shortcuts to having a happy and rewarding life—but I have discovered many tips to keeping myself on track.

Here are my words to live by. If you don't have the haters, you're not doing it right. (Bobby Brown told me these words of wisdom when we filmed *Celebrity Fit Club*, and I thank him for it on a daily basis.) Put your money and education before your emotions. Basing your career decisions around a specific lifestyle will only make you end up looking broke and stupid. Pick the people that you love and keep them by your side. Let the rest fend for themselves. Facts and feelings usually aren't the same. Actually, they are pretty much never the same. Don't just argue your emotions—think about WHAT IS. Stop trying to be friends with unstable people! Eventually they will pull you down. It's a beautiful thing to stay silent when someone expects you to be enraged. Not everyone has to like you. Not everyone has taste. Don't give everyone a chance to get to know you. I know a shitload of people but very few get the privilege of *really* knowing me. I promise it's not shade—it's being selective. Not everyone needs to be close and I prefer it that way. Take the time for you. Take that yoga class, go to the spa, read a good book. Remember that behind every successful woman is HERSELF.

CHAPTER 19

The (Mostly) Happy Ending

After all of this reflection, am I still Fed up and Tired?

Yes…and no.

The other day, my niece Kaydence asked me if I wanted to go to Arendelle, the kingdom in the movie *Frozen*.

"Shoot, Kaydence," I said. "I wish Arendelle really existed. I'd sure like to bag a handsome prince!"

Would it be nice if we could all live in a magical kingdom?

I would be lying if I said I don't have voids in my life. I'm still looking for that magical knight in shining armor, although I realize that he doesn't have to be perfect on paper to love and accept me for who I am.

I hope to be a mother in the near future. I'm learning to recognize that being a parent might not involve a perfect marriage. I almost promised my parents I wouldn't have kids out of wedlock, but when time starts to run out I might start to change my mind. I look at pictures of my friends' kids and I feel that ache. I want to plan birthday parties and play dress up. I want to play hide and seek and have food fights one day too. All in due time, I guess.

One day I would love to host my own talk show. There are certain things in life you cannot teach. You just have to have it. I didn't think hosting was my thing, but now I'm confident as a host. I *love* what I do. I have this innate connection with people. I can connect with the shiest person in the room, I can deliver the truth with tough love, I can keep it real and tell you how it is without breaking you down. And I love making people laugh.

I knew my life would change the moment I got picked for *Bad Girls Club*. Never did I think that I would still be working in this industry almost ten years later, successful in many endeavors. I could have been pigeonholed as a Bad Girl for the rest of my career, but with hard work and lots of help I have been able to evolve and grow. I've proven that I am smart, business-savvy, and a good role model. The support that people have shown me is amazing and has enabled me to turn a reality TV platform into an empire. I'm blessed and I'm thankful and I'm humble.

Do I want to give up sometimes? Honey, I quit *every damn day*. I think I quit every hour—I think I quit today! But every time I come across a new roadblock and want to give up, I focus on the long term I ask myself, "What is the bigger picture and how can I get there?" I set these goals for myself and no matter how upset I get, no matter how stressful it gets, I am determined to make sure I follow through. Even if I fall flat on my face, it's important for me to say, "You know what? At least I tried!"

What keeps me moving is the knowledge that this journey I'm on isn't my doing. I didn't arrive here by luck or chance. I firmly believe that I was chosen for this life, as a vessel to connect to so many of you. I am grateful for all of my blessings, and opportunities, and although life can really throw me some curveballs, I understand to whom much is given much is required.

My life is far from perfect, but this is what I've learned: At some point you have to let go of what you thought should happen and live in what is happening. I've dealt with so much in my life and I know what it's like to be knocked down and to hit rock bottom. I use everything that life has thrown at me, and I apply it in every single situation.

I've built a career from scratch, and I've grown and evolved and come into my own. I feel new and improved and amazing. And even if I haven't sorted everything out, I understand the importance of patience.

I'm here for the journey.

About the Author

Tanisha Thomas is the hilarious, larger-than-life Brooklyn diva and television host with an extensive background in various reality television. She currently resides in her hometown, Brooklyn, New York.